5 -

Kosciuszko and Pulaski

Jan Stanisław Kopczewski

Kosciuszko and Pulaski

Interpress Publishers, Warsaw 1976

Contents

Chapter I

Kosciuszko and Pulaski Two Portraits

It was America that brought the names of Thaddeus Kosciuszko and Casimir Pulaski together, but only in the posthumous glory they were both to share. Although they had both been in America at the same time and both had fought for America's independence, their individual destinies unfolded in such a manner that in all likelihood they never met. Since the roads they had traveled earlier in their native Poland and subsequently in France also never seemed to converge, it appears safe to assume that Kosciuszko and Pulaski — whose names are now uttered in a single breath in connexion with Poland's and America's joint traditions of struggle for independence — never became personally acquainted.

Still, for many years tradition held that they had indeed met in December 1777 at Trenton, New Jersey. Such an episode was contained in the memoirs — published in Paris in 1847 — of Pulaski's personal friend and comrade-in-arms, the cavalry captain Maciej Rogowski. This is how he described that alleged meeting:

"It happened that towards the end of December, at Christmastime, we were in for a delightful surprise. Thaddeus Kosciuszko, who was serving as an engineer with the northern army near the Canadian frontier, decided while on furlough to honor us with a visit, having learnt that Pulaski was in Trenton. Kosciuszko lacked Casimir's pugnacious countenance, but he radiated honesty and noble candor, whilst being a most affable soul always full of news; we therefore found his company and discourses most pleasurable. Although Kosciuszko was the same age as Pulaski, they had not known each other in Poland; the former had been poring over his books, whilst the latter was already teaching the Russians a lesson. Thus it was here, on foreign soil, that a bond of deep affection between them was established, as they pledged each other undying friendship. After ten days of merry-making during which — despite our impoverished state — we strove to do justice to our festive Old Polish traditions — Kosciuszko took leave of us to rejoin his corps..."

The above narrative, having all the appearance of an authentic document, turned out to be apocryphal, skillful and credible fabrication by the writer and poet Konstanty Gaszyński, whose name had figured on the title page as the publisher of these discovered fragments of a genuine set of memoirs. This not only confused novelist Józef Ignacy Kraszewski who — on the basis of the above description — penned a beautiful scene of the meeting at Trenton in his novel *The Wanderers*, but also succeeded in misleading Professor Tadeusz Korzon, the author of the most exhaustive biography of Kosciuszko to date, published in 1894. Later researchers were to question the authenticity of Rogowski's memoirs, for in minutely tracing the roads traveled by the two heroes in America, they were unable to establish the place and date of the alleged meeting.

Although a meeting at Trenton is not ruled out, no actual evidence of its occurrence has ever been provided. The fact remains, however, that in the letters of Pulaski and Kosciuszko (as well as in other contemporary writings) there is no mention of their mutual acquaintance. It may have seemed plausible that they should meet when both simultaneously found themselves on the opposite side of the Atlantic. While still in Poland, Kosciuszko must have heard of Pulaski, the renowned commander of the Bar Confederation; by contrast, Pulaski may not have heard of Kosciuszko, since it was only in America that his name gradually began to gain prominence. From the above it would appear that the question as to whether they knew each other must be answered negatively. On the other hand, it is unknown whether they had ever heard about each other. The fact remains that their names have been linked by tradition in the annals of history. In keeping with that tradition, this book is concerned with both heroes and consequently we should begin by determining what, besides their American episode, they had in common and what set them apart or even at variance with each other.

There was hardly any age difference between them: Kosciuszko was born on 4 February 1746, Pulaski on 4 March 1747. Both were of gentle birth, though Pulaski's was the wealthier family. With a mixture of adroitness and enterprise, Pulaski's father succeeded in multiplying the family fortune many times over. Subsequently it was confiscated for a time after the Bar Confederation had been crushed in 1772 and it never returned to its former splendor. By contrast, the modest estate which Kosciuszko had inherited from his father did not produce any income to speak of. As a result, once in America neither of them had any family fortune to fall back on. The title of count, which the Americans frequently bestowed upon them (Pulaski often used it himself), indicated merely noble birth and not riches.

Both Pulaski and Kosciuszko considered their service in the American army as a voluntary involvement and neither sought any material gains from it. Pulaski never received any sums for his own expenses, and Kosciuszko's army pay — like that of other American commanders — was not calculated until after the war. The money he eventually did receive Kosciuszko set aside for the emancipation of American Negroes.

It would be an exaggeration to state that both of them fought for American independence out of commitment to republican ideals. Their personal destinies had compelled them to seek glory on a battlefield far from their homeland. They chose a country from which "the voice of freedom" had issued forth — a country trying to throw off the yoke of foreign domination. Among Poles, whose country was then threatened by the total loss of sovereignty, that slogan evoked a feeling of solidarity.

Kosciuszko, who displayed an affinity with those groups in France which were laying the groundwork for revolution, was stirred not only by efforts to liberate America from British subjugation but also by the republican character of the movement. Pulaski, by contrast, was a soldier rather than an ideologist. As one of the commanders of the Bar Confederation he had simply fought for the freedom of his homeland without endorsing any specific socio-political program. He had, however, been embroiled in a confederate plot to abduct the king of Poland, and as one who had dared to raise his hand against the monarch he was sentenced to death *in absentia*. Pulaski's involvement in that plot had stemmed from the belief that the Polish king was selling his country out to foreign powers, notably Russia. Although Pulaski's part in this anti-royalist conspiracy might have increased his standing in republican circles, he chose not to take advantage of that fact. But his reputation as an outstanding commander of the confederate forces in 1768—72 enabled him to achieve the rank of cavalry general a year and a half after his arrival in America. Kosciuszko turned up in America without any battlefield experience. He did not take part in the confederate struggle, as at that time he was pursuing military studies in Paris. He had gone there to study under a scholarship provided by King Stanislaus Augustus Poniatowski, whom the Bar Confederation had sought to dethrone and Pulaski's men attempted to abduct. Had the Americans wanted to test the "republicanism" of the two candidates as a criterion of admission to Washington's army, Kosciuszko's chances would have been considerably slimmer. But the people engaged in recruiting volunteers for America in Paris were concerned mainly with the military skills of prospective candidates and with the opinion they enjoyed among French politicians favorably disposed to the American nation's struggle for independence. Both Poles found Frenchmen willing to vouch for them. Kosciuszko had an easier time of it, however, and arrived in the New World earlier than Pulaski who spent nine months vainly endeavoring to reach America. Kosciuszko's advantage in receiving an assignment from the American army, which suffered a dire lack of qualified specialists, was his thorough education as a military engineer. For that very reason, shortly after his arrival in Philadelphia, he received the rank of engineer colonel. He was among the first European officers to be recruited, arriving in America most probably in July or August 1776, nearly a year earlier than Pulaski.

The nature of the functions the two Poles performed was completely different. During his first four years Engineer Colonel Kosciuszko was busy designing and supervising the construction of fortifications (Philadelphia, Ticonderoga, Saratoga, West Point). His greatest claim to fame during that period was his contribution to the American victory in the Battle of Saratoga (17 October 1777), as attested to by General Horatio Gates. Kosciuszko had been charged with selecting the correct position for the army prior to the battle and constructing the requisite field fortifications. Those and later achievements of Kosciuszko failed to receive the acknowledgement they deserved in the eyes of the commander-in-chief, George Washington, because the Polish colonel was generally considered to be " Gates' man " — Gates being one of Washington's antagonists. If to this one adds Kosciuszko's shyness, modesty, reserve and lack of diplomatic finesse, it is easy to understand why he remained in the background. He was promoted to the post of chief engineer in the southern army only after his predecessor, a Frenchman, had been captured by the enemy. And he did not become a general until after the war had ended.

Kosciuszko did not find himself in the southern theater of the war, where Pulaski had fought and fallen in battle in 1779, until a year after the latter's death. The 12th of December 1782 was an important day in Kosciuszko's life, for it marked both the end and the culmination of his service to America. That was the day of his triumphal march at the head of the first American troops to enter Charleston after the British surrender. That honor was extended to him in recognition of his contribution to the southern campaign led by General Nathanael Greene. In the same town Pulaski had fought at the head of his legion in May 1779, and it was there that a symbolic funeral ceremony with full military honors was held for the hero of Savannah six months later (his mortal remains had been buried at sea, for he had died aboard a brig en route from Savannah to Charleston).

If one were to single out a locality in the United States where the battle trails of Kosciuszko and Pulaski had indeed met (though at different times and under different circumstances), the most likely choice would be Charleston. That would be the most appropriate site for a monument in honor of the two heroes.

Pulaski's American episode had been linked to the person of George Washington. Unlike Kosciuszko, the general commanding the cavalry had kept in close contact with Washington who seemed to have a personal liking for the mettlesome if occasionally somewhat refractory and capricious Pole. That is amply attested to by Washington's consent to and support (contrary to the views of Congress) for the creation of a special unit, the Pulaski Legion, whose guerrilla nature was superbly suited to the temperament of its commander. Pulaski's US army career could therefore be termed successful, were it not for the fact that military successes as such seemed to pass him by. Using battle drills he himself had developed, Pulaski put all he had into the training of American, Irish and German dragoons and turned them into an efficient arm capable of carrying out independent military actions. For, ever true to his native tradition, that is how the Polish nobleman viewed the role of the cavalry, unlike the Americans who only made use of small mounted units mainly for reconnaissance missions. Thus, although he did not fight any major, victorious battle, Pulaski was to go down in US military history as " the father of the American cavalry". He died heroically and won a permanent place among the heroes of the American War of Independence. His display of courage and dedication at the Battle of Savannah (9 October 1779) has not been forgotten.

Kosciuszko's merits were not recalled until after the war. Besides a much delayed promotion to the rank of general (13 October 1783), he was accorded yet another distinction: the Order of the Cincinnati, which marked his admission into an exclusive society affiliating the most distinguished participants in the struggle for American independence. Numerous portraits depict Kosciuszko wearing this decoration together with the Polish military order of Virtuti Militari which he was to receive nine years later.

Such in general outline were the American exploits of the two heroes. Despite the different roads each of them traveled, they have both gone down in the history of the American Revolution as comrades-in-arms, joined by a single idea for which they fought under a common banner.

Let us now take a closer look at the services of Kosciuszko and Pulaski to their own Polish homeland with a view to what they may have had in common, despite the undeniable differences that set them apart.

It has often been said that Pulaski was a representative of the traditional, pre-partition Poland of the gentry, unlike Kosciuszko who personified a new emerging Poland, which was being forged into a single nation in the fire of the struggle to liberate the homeland.

The Bar Confederation was a patriotic movement, based on the conservative ideology of the gentry. The confederates rose in defense of " faith and freedom" in 1768, but it was to be that "golden freedom" which did not tolerate any restrictions (on the gentry) imposed by strengthened royal or parliamentary authority. That brand of freedom as exemplified by the *liberum veto* (whereby a single dissenting deputy could dissolve the Seym) had brought great harm to the country. The freedom enjoyed by the gentry, together with the weakness of the Seym and the king, had provided the great landowners with untold opportunities to buy support and to conduct their own policies contrary to national interests. The slogan of defending the Catholic faith, put forward in response to parliamentary acts extending equal rights to religious dissenters, was intended to rally the traditionally Catholic gentry, known for their intolerance towards other denominations. In this way the leaders of the Confederation sought to impart to their movement the character of a religious war. This, in the period of the Enlightenment, was an anachronism.

Kosciuszko's ideology stood in marked contrast to this. His famous words uttered on the eve of the insurrection : " I shall not fight for the gentry alone ; I desire the freedom of the entire nation !" — clearly indicated his progressive, modern way of thinking. It is true that the official motto of the insurrection " Freedom, Integrity [i.e. territorial integrity — ed. note], Independence" was somewhat more ambivalent than that of the Republicans : " Freedom, Equality, Fraternity". And yet, his famous Proclamation at Połaniec, which ensured the peasantry personal freedom and curtailed serfdom, indicated that Kosciuszko had indeed favored the equality of all citizens. But since he also sought to rally the conservative elements of Polish society to the cause (the gentry, after all, constituted the main military force), Kosciuszko had to play down the revolutionary nature of the insurrection. The keeping of the king from having any influence on the course of the insurrection, while retaining the monarchy as such also represented a compromise. Kosciuszko was, therefore, no Jacobin, for under the circumstances of the 1794 insurrection that was impossible. He was, however, a republican, an adherent of the social concepts of the Enlightenment.

It is more difficult to ascertain Pulaski's ideological position during the period of the Bar Confederation. He was a soldier first and foremost, and there is nothing to indicate that he had had a hand in formulating the confederation's ideology. His father, Józef Pulaski, had been one of the founders of the movement. Casimir, who was 21 when the confederation came into being, simply followed in his father's footsteps. It should also be remembered that the confederation's ideology underwent a major evolution in the space of four years. Suffice it to say that in a war which had originally been initiated in defense of the Catholic faith, dissenters were later to take part both in a military and a political capacity. Religious slogans were emblazoned on the banners borne by the confederates, but that fact was without major significance. And the original slogan calling for the restoration of "golden freedom" was eventually transformed into a struggle for national independence. Many burghers and peasants were also to be found in the ranks of the Confederation, and a considerable group of former confederates later went on to become framers and champions of the Constitution of 3 May. Hence, it would be pointless categorically to juxtapose members of the Bar Confederation with Kosciuszko's insurrectionists. It should also be remembered that a quarter of a century had elapsed between the formation of the confederation at Bar and the proclamation of the Kosciuszko Insurrection. In the meantime revolutionary France had emerged on the international scene, marking the dawn of a new era in European history.

Had he lived till 1794, Pulaski would undoubtedly have rallied to Kosciuszko's standard as did a number of other former confederates. They strengthened the officer cadre of the Insurrection, and without declaring themselves either for or against universal equality, they fought for independence as they had in the past.

Whatever may be said of the social nature of the Confederation or the Kosciuszko movement, the fact remains that their overriding aim was to throw off the foreign yoke and restore independence. The battle cry "death or victory" accompanied the banners of the Confederation only to be later adopted by the soldiers of Kosciuszko. It was that slogan of struggle for independence which was common to both our heroes, and it was for that ideal too that they both fought on foreign soil. But only one of them was to return to raise that banner in his own country when the latter was threatened with imminent loss of independence.

It may be said, therefore, that the roads they traveled, though frequently divergent, led to a single objective, but they did not lead to an encounter between Kosciuszko and Pulaski behind the same barricade. A knowledge of their early years explains why one of them was studying military engineering abroad on a royal scholarship, whilst the other was waging a struggle against Russia and a Polish monarch subservient to that country. The history of the Bar Confederation shows the great role it played in kindling a spirit of resistance which would subsequently engulf the entire nation during the Kosciuszko Insurrection. And although they were never to meet personally, their American sojourn proved that they both earned the honorable title of "fighters for the freedom of peoples". It is not surprising, therefore, that both their likenesses were engraved on a common commemorative medal bearing the inscription : *Kosciuszko et Pulaski populorum libertatis milites.*

On the other hand, in our search for what they had in common, we shall not attempt to blur the differences that set them apart nor try to create a single, synthetic image to fit both heroes. For, while it is true that in an American context the names of Kosciuszko and Pulaski may be uttered in the same breath, each of them occupied his own distinct place in the pantheon of Polish history. On the Polish scene Pulaski was to play his major role as a young man in his twenties prior to the partitions. It was only a quarter of a century later that the 48-year-old Kosciuszko would emerge to set the stage for a new epoch in the course of a 200-day insurrection.

If one approaches the Polish activities of both heroes in this manner, the person of Casimir Pulaski may be seen to form a part of a bygone era which ended with the partitions of Poland, whilst pointing out the road to freedom for those who would follow. The person of Thaddeus Kosciuszko, by contrast, emerged at the threshold of a new stage in national history, foreshadowing the birth of a new Poland. Though Pulaski and Kosciuszko were joined by the common idea of struggle for Poland's independence, the different periods and circumstances in which each of them was to function gave their activities a different dimension and a separate place in the history of their homeland.

12

"Kosciuszko and Pulaski — fighters for the freedom of peoples".
A medal struck in 1876 on the centenary of the US Decla-
ration of Independence to commemorate the contri-
butions of the two Poles to the struggle
for America's freedom; the reverse
depicts George Washington

13

19th-century portraits of Thaddeus Kosciuszko and Casimir Pulaski, the best-known likenesses of the two heroes, executed in the steel-engraving technique by the outstanding portraitist, Antoni Oleszczyński

14

15

Casimir Pulaski as a member of the Bar Confederation (after a 19th century lithograph)

19th-century medallions portraying Casimir Pulaski and Thaddeus Kosciuszko

18

KOSCIUSZKO

Grabowicz. del.   [De la Coll.ᵒⁿ de L. Chodźko.]   James Hopwood, sc

KASIMIR PULASKI

Maréchal de la Terre de Lomza dans le Palatinat de Mazovie, en 1768

Chef militaire de la Confédération de Bar de 1769 à 1772

Général de cavalerie sous les ordres de Washington en 1777

Commandant la légion étrangère au service des Etats-Unis de l'Amérique du Nord en 1779

Né à Winiary près d'Ostróg le 4 Mars 1748.

Mort au siège de Savannah en Georgie le 9 Octobre 1779

20

[De la Coll.ⁿ de Léonard Chodzko]

James Hopwood sc.

THADÉ KOSCIUSZKO.

Elève de l'école militaire ou Corps des cadets de Warsovie.

Général aux armées des États Unis de l'Amérique du Nord, commandées par Washington.

Generalissime, avec les pouvoirs dictatoriaux de toutes les forces nationales polonaises et lithuaniennes en 1794.

Né à Mereczowszczyzna en Lithuanie le 12 février 1746.

Mort à Soleure en Suisse le 15 Octobre 1817.

SLAWNI I ZASLUZENI POLACY.

Pleiad of great Poles (19th-century lithograph); from top to bottom: Prince Mieszko I and King Boleslaus the Brave, King Casimir the Great, King John Sobieski, King Sigismund the Old, Royal Commander Stefan Czarniecki, Thaddeus Kosciuszko, Casimir Pulaski, Prince Józef Poniatowski, Nicolaus Copernicus, Piotr Skarga, Joachim Lelewel, Frédéric Chopin, Juliusz Słowacki, Adam Mickiewicz, Zygmunt Krasiński and Karol Marcinkowski. (The latter was a physician and civic leader in the Great Poland region, which apparently entitled him to be ranked among this anyway quite random selection by a Poznań publisher of seventeen outstanding Poles)

19th-century albums of outstanding Poles generally included Kosciuszko and often Pulaski, as well. These two figures exemplified the famous Polish battle cry "For Our Freedom and Yours". Below: a medallion of Kosciuszko and Pulaski executed through the efforts of the Americans of Polish origin in the late 19th-century

KOŚCIUSZKO TADEUSZ

KAZIMIERZ PUŁAWSKI

Kazimierz Pułaski

There is a relatively small number of portraits of Pulaski, and those that do exist are quite similar both in terms of facial characteristics and attire (cf. the portraits on preceding pages and on pp. 97, 104, 118 and 119). This is not the case with Kosciuszko's portraits which are quite varied as may be seen from those presented on the following pages, many of which appeared during his lifetime. By contrast no contemporary portrait of Pulaski has survived. Among the earliest was the oil portrait dating from the beginning of the 19th century which is presented here

KAZIMIERZ PUŁAWSKI

Dowódca w Konfederacyi Barskiey
Generał jazdy Stanów zjednoczonych Ameryki

26

Thaddeus Kosciuszko as a knight in armor (although he naturally never donned such attire), painted in Warsaw in 1792 by Josef Grassi, a well-known Viennese artist. The tranquil facial expression was to serve as a pattern for many later portraits (compare reproduction on p. 21).

This aquatint, executed in Paris in 1794, was known as "Kosciuszko's Jacobin portrait". The border inscription reads: "He never raised his arm in the defense of kings; he became a conqueror of despotism in both hemispheres". Depicted above the portrait is a Phrygian cap, symbol of the French Revolution

TADÉE KOSCIUSZKO

Par ses vertus, ses Talens
et la confiance du Peuple
Chef de la force armée nationale
de Pologne, contre les sattelites des
Brigands couronnés.

le 24 Mars, 1794.

A Paris chez Guyot Graveur, rue Jacques N.9.

27

Thaddeus Kosciuszko as a general of the Polish army (probably painted prior to 1792 as the absence of the Virtuti Militari medal would suggest); next to it: the earliest example of an extensive series portraying Kosciuszko with a saber (Paris, May 1793)

KOSCIUSZKO *Célebre général Polonois, réfugié en France en 1793 et faisant actuellement la révolution de Pologne.*

Dess. au Physionotrace en 1793 par Quenedey.

Pozwol ieszcze raz bic sie za | *Fais que je puisse me battre*
Oyczyzne. | *encore une fois pour ma patrie.*

Se vend chez Quenedey, rue Croix des Petits Champs N°s 10 et 81 a Paris.

29

The "Portrait with Saber" in 1794 became the official image of the leader of the insurrection and was frequently copied abroad in Germany, Holland, Britain and France. The type of saber shown in these portraits later became known as a "Kosciuszkówka"

KOSCIUSZKO.

GAZETA
POWSTANIA POLSKI.

NRO. 5.

29. Kwietnia
Roku 1794.

w Warszawie
w Drukarni na
Krakows: Przed-
mieściu Nro: 380.
przeciw Poczty.
Przez Tadeusza
Podleckiego.

TADEUSZ KOSCIUSZKO
Naywyższy Naczelnik siły zbroyney
NARODU POLSKIEGO.

DO TEGO PORTRETU.

Oto iest żywy Portret Naywyższego teraznieyszego Naczelnika Siły
Zbroyney Narodu Polskiego, który że iest prawdziwie trafiony nad wszystkie insze Ryfunki, tak powszechnie uznaią, iakim Go widzieli w Oryginale
po skończoney przeszłey Woynie. Oto iest wyobrażenie tego, Który dał
dowody i Zdatności i Meftwa swoiego na Woynie Amerykańskiey, o czym
od całego Świata niezaprzeczona dotąd ftoi prawda. — Który potym po-
wróciwszy do fwey Oyczyzny, gdy się pora otworzyła ratowania Jéy, zo-
ftawszy tylko Generał-Majorem, czegoż nie dokazywał? mianowicie pod
Dubienką, w kilka tyfięcy Woyfka, przeciwko kilkunastu tyfięcy Mofkwy,
a ieszcze przy Ordynanfie cofania się, jak wiadomo, że cała tamta Kampa-
nia, była tylko cofaiąca fię. Który i teraz przy famym iuż konaniu fwey
Oyczyzny, pierwfzy porwał się ią ratować w dniu 24. Marca Roku tera-
zieyfzego, i gdyby był nie pospieszył, iużby był dotąd Jéy pogrzeb.
                                                F
                                                Żeby

Kosciuszko in a peasant coat and a "liberty cap", as depicted by Josef Grassi and subsequently often imitated, was the standard portrayal of the commander of the peasant scythebearers. This portrait, with its rich symbolism (revolutionary cap, peasant coat, rays of sunshine emerging from the clouds) was copied in many versions, not only by Polish, but also by French, German, Swedish and Russian artists.

Sketches by Aleksander Orłowski, who took part in the insurrection at the age of 16, give a quite different view of Kosciuszko; most likely done from the life, their freedom reveals the latent talent of someone destined to become a great painter

32

The cult surrounding the commander of the insurrection had already given rise to numerous miniatures by the end of the 18th century and they continued to appear on through the 19th century. The earliest and most valuable are those painted by Jan Rustem, depicting Kosciuszko in profile, dressed in a frock-coat. Many miniatures portrayed Kosciuszko in general's uniform; the mini-portrait showing Kosciuszko in a peasant coat dates from c. 1863

GENERAL KOSCIUSKO.

Published as the Act directs February 1ʸᵗ 1795, by Verner & Hood Birchen Lane Cornhill.

Many portraits painted by foreign artists, even contemporaries of Kosciuszko, bore little resemblance (moustache, wig!) to the Polish hero; the attire, in which the subject was portrayed, was also quite randomly chosen. Besides highly idealized portraits, images bordering on caricatures could also be found

Kosciuszko (signature)

Thadé kosciuszko né a Brzecs en Lithuanie; agé d'un
inquante ans grand général de la confédération
...... puis le 10 8bre 1794 par le corps Russe. a
.... en général ......

KOSCIVSKO
General en Chef des Polonnois.

Kosciuszko. (signature)

THADDEUS KOSCIUSZKO

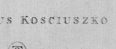

GENERAL KOSCIUSKO.
Commander in chief of the Polish Army.

The fame of the leader of Poland's insurrection ensured Kosciuszko a place among the eight outstanding commanders, jointly portrayed on a lithograph by a French artist specializing in military scenes.

Many battle scenes, painted during the firs half of thd 19th century, failed to portray Kosciuszko in either an authentic or competentt manner

39

The hero of the Battle of Racławice was honored by many amateur artists, whose allegorical portrayals often move the beholder by their naiveté

The second half of the 19th century witnessed a spate of new portrayals of Kosciuszko as well as imitations of older portraits, which combined various elements of dress, e.g. a general's uniform with a peasant coat slung over the shoulders, and the traditional Polish our-cornered hat adorning the hero's head

KOŚCIUSZKO.

41

A frequently recurring motif on many paintings and engravings portrayed Kosciuszko at Maciejowice falling from his steed a moment before being taken into captivity. It was also found on a crystal cup produced by a Bohemian glass-works in the mid-19th century

44

During the insurrection silhouettes of Kosciuszko adorned the belts and cartridge pouches of Polish soldiers. This motif also appeared on Polish porcelain in the late 18th century. The silver belt buckle adorned with two rows of crystals bears the inscription "O Pole, if you have feelings, weep over the fate of the Resurrector of Freedom", which shows that it was used after the collapse of the Insurrection in 1794. An unusual memento of the Kosciuszko cult was a series of paper cut-outs, executed by a participant of the insurrection, allegorically portraying the history of the insurrection

Numerous creations of 19th-century artisans such as jewelry, snuffboxes, clocks etc., featured the image of Kosciuszko

46

A medal depicting Kosciuszko, Pulaski and Washington, struck in 1926 on the 150th anniversary of the Declaration of Independence; it was patterned after a medal executed in 1876 (see reproduction on p. 13)

Chapter II

The Land of Their Youth

In Polish history the 18th century is a period of great contrasts. While it was a century of general political, economic and cultural decline, it also witnessed genuinely remarkable achievements in each of those fields. Amid symptoms of stagnation and decay there appeared increasingly visible signs of the country's rebirth in the spirit of reforms which rejected everything that retarded socio-economic development and constituted a negative legacy of bygone epochs.

The two main tendencies of the period were a conservative and reactionary trend opposed to any and all changes which might jeopardize the position of the privileged strata — the gentry and the magnates — and a trend towards renewal, which sought ways to overcome the general atrophy. The latter was orientated towards the development of the state and society as set forth by the most outstanding minds of the Enlightenment. The conflict between those two orientations determined the main line of Poland's internal development in the 18th century.

The external factors determining Poland's destiny presented quite a different picture. The shape of European relations in the 18th century was not generally favorable to the Polish cause. Penetration by the big powers, whose influence sought to weaken Poland, was conducive to the spread of anarchy. And three successive partitions (1772, 1793, 1795) finally succeeded in wiping the Polish state off the map of Europe.

The 18th century might have appeared to spell the definitive end of eight centuries of Polish statehood as well as the undoing of all that was achieved during the final decades preceding the catastrophe. Years later, however, the outcome of that balance-sheet would turn out quite differently. The ideas contained in state reforms (the Constitution of 3 May, 1791), in the socio-political literature of that period and, finally, in the armed movements in defense of independence, would enable a nation, deprived of its own state from 1795 to 1918, to endure 123 years of subjugation. And not only endure, for in the interim it made the transition from a "nation of the privileged strata" to a modern nation combining all social strata and classes in a single organism.

Particularly important were the final three decades of freedom, when amidst ignorance and obscurantism enlightened ideas began to flare up; when amidst symptoms of political degeneration there emerged a sweeping program of governmental reform within the framework of a new constitution; when signs of general economic stagnation were countered by the emergence of new forms of economic organization; when, in the face of the country's military collapse, the sacrifice of its citizens and their readiness to defend their homeland, its "freedom, integrity and independence" came to the fore. This slogan, which would form the substance of the Polish nation's existence from the end of the 18th century down to the present, emerged in the mid-18th century and was first used by Stanisław Konarski, one of the precursors of Poland's Age of Enlightenment. Even the song of 1797 which begins with the words "Poland has not yet perished as long as we are alive" (and is now Poland's official national anthem) came into being at a time when the old Polish state was collapsing and a modern nation was emerging.

In speaking of the contrasts, the opposing currents and the ups and downs of Polish life in the 18th century it should be remembered that the beginning of the 18th century and its final years were completely different periods. Roughly speaking, the century may be divided into a "Saxon period" and a "Stanislavian period". Up till 1763 Poland was ruled by the Saxon Dynasty: King Augustus II (1697—1733) and his son, Augustus III. Twice during that period (in 1704 and 1733) Stanislaus Leszczyński, an opponent of the Saxons, who was supported by the progressive section of Polish society, tried to seize the throne. He had been elected king of Poland at first with Swedish help and on the second occasion with French help. But the Russian support extended to the two successive Saxon monarchs proved stronger. The successor of Augustus III was another protégé of the Russians, Stanislaus Augustus Poniatowski. The fact that monarchs, supported by foreign interests, ascended the Polish throne attested to the internal weakness of a country that in bygone periods had exerted its own influence on other European governments.

One politician during the latter half of the 18th century called the Polish Kingdom under the Saxons "a roadside inn" where anybody with money and power could rule. 18th century Poland, however, had neither money nor military might. Foreign armies penetrated the country without even meeting with resistance. Poland became embroiled in the Northern War (1700—21) waged by Denmark and Russia against Sweden, as the Saxon Augustus II had hoped in this way to acquire Livonia for his dynasty. It would have been more in Poland's interest to weaken Russia, instead of waging war on Sweden. As a result, large parts of Polish territory became a battlefield for the foreign armies of Sweden and Saxony, leading to devastation and pillage. A similar situation arose in 1733. After the death of Augustus II and the election of Stanislaus Leszczyński to the Polish throne, Saxon and Russian armies entered Poland to ensure the accession of the Saxon Augustus III to the throne. For the third time Poland became a "roadside inn" for foreign armies, this time the Russian and Prussian armies engaged in the Seven Years War (1756—63).

The reason for Poland's defenselessness was the total decline of military organization during the Saxon period. The military exploits of King John III Sobieski (who defeated the Turks at Chocim in 1673 and Vienna in 1683) had become a thing of the past. The general disintegration and the decline of patriotism, together with a depleted royal treasury, made it impossible to rebuild Poland's armed forces which had become all but an anachronism by the beginning of the 18th century. Not only in terms of troop strength but also as regards its level of training and armament the Polish army was no match for those of Sweden, Prussia, Russia, Saxony or Austria. In 1717 the Seym was pressured by the Russians into limiting Poland's armed forces to 24,000 men, but in the decades that followed even that level was not achieved.

Poland's economy was in catastrophic shape under the Saxon Dynasty. The reasons for this, besides the devastation and pillage wrought by wars, included natural disasters, exceptionally poor harvests and epidemics. But the main reason for the sorry state of affairs was the overall backwardness of the economy. Only a handful of owners of huge landed estates began to introduce taxation, whereas the general rule of the day was compulsory peasant labor, the amount of which was arbitrarily increased by the landlords as prices climbed. The system of farming and the agricultural implements employed were primitive, the poverty-stricken serf worked inefficiently and much land lay fallow. The country's war-ravaged and depopulated towns were in no position properly to stimulate the development of trade and crafts.

For the vast majority of Poland's inhabitants the Saxon period was a time of poverty. It was a difficult period for the semi-affluent gentry as well. In those lawless times the more impoverished minor gentry were drawn to and sought the patronage of powerful landed aristocrats who could afford to maintain their own armies. The great manors not only grew in influence but also increased their wealth. Amidst general poverty huge fortunes were acquired, only to be subsequently squandered at times in an unprecedented manner.

Public life for which the nobility had once displayed such enthusiasm, now experienced a period of visible regression. Assemblies of the gentry became occasions for powerful aristocrats to gain supporters, elections of deputies to the Seym were conducted in accordance with the instructions of local magnates and the participation of the gentry masses in the governing processes more often involved dissolving parliament than adopting constructive legislation. Not a single session of parliament in the years 1736—63 succeeded in completing its debates. Deputies, acting in the interests of their aristocratic patrons or bribed by foreign powers, would dissolve a parliamentary session on the basis of the anachronistic right of *liberum veto*. Under the circumstances, participation by the gentry in government was all but fictitious. Those who really counted were the magnates. It was they who exercised influence at the court of the Polish king or, even worse, at the courts of neighboring powers which viewed the decline of Poland as an opportunity to fish in troubled waters.

Such is the image of the Saxon reign which comes into focus from the perspective of the two centuries that now separate us from that period of collapsing statehood and overall social stagnation. But even then progressive political writers were aware of the existing state of affairs. In the latter half of the 18th century Stanisław Konarski was the first to initiate a great patriotic debate on the improvement of the Commonwealth, and between 1761 and 1763 he published a work entitled *A Way to Effective Councils*. In it he criticized the defects of Poland's policy, called for the elimination of the *liberum veto* and spoke out in favor of strengthening the authority of the Seym. In an earlier treatise, *On Ensuring the Happiness of One's Own Homeland* (1757) Konarski had defended the interests of the peasantry and the burgher class.

During the final quarter of the century, as the ideals of the Enlightenment gained new adherents in Poland, calls for reform were heard from such outstanding political figures, scholars and writers as Hugo Kołłątaj, Stanisław Staszic, Ignacy Krasicki and Julian Ursyn Niemcewicz.

It was thus in quite a different atmosphere that Stanislaus Augustus Poniatowski ascended the throne in 1764. Although the Constitution of 3 May — the greatest legislative achievement of pre-partition Poland and a tribute to the political maturity of the reformist camp — would not be promulgated until 27 years later, voices calling for the reorganization of the internally weak and anarchical homeland were already making themselves heard at the outset of the Stanislavian period. The political program of the Czartoryski faction, which had advanced the candidacy of Poniatowski after the death of Augustus III, envisaged the modernization and strengthening of state authority. But in 1764 it was still too early to introduce any actual changes, since the bulk of the gentry, especially the magnates representing mainly conservative views, would have deemed this to be a blow against the "golden freedom" of the nobility.

The coronation of the Czartoryskis' candidate had been made possible not because of their reform program, but rather owing to the support of Catherine II of Russia. Foreign meddling in Polish affairs did not cease. On the contrary, the entire reign of the last Polish king was marked by ever more menacing instances of intervention from without. Russia, which in 1717 had usurped the right to act as a "guarantor" vis-à-vis Poland, began increasingly to subordinate the latter to her dictates. In the north and west a threat was posed by Prussia's greed for conquest. Thus, despite certain manifestations of internal reform both in the economic realm as well as public involvement, the threat of ultimate loss of independence and statehood hung over Poland from the very beginning of the Stanislavian period. The collapse of the Polish state occurred in the 31st year of the reign of Stanislaus Augustus Poniatowski and was sealed by the treaty of partition of 1795.

Armed resistance such as the Bar Confederation in 1768 and the Kosciuszko Insurrection of 1794 proved incapable of saving the country. But they did succeed in engendering a spirit of struggle and prevented the Polish nation from losing faith in its right to independence. To the post-partition generations both the struggle of the Bar confederates including the feats of their most famous leader Casimir Pulaski and the Kosciuszko Insurrection became models deserving of emulation and pride, a heroic epic of a sinking though immortal nation. Historians must naturally assess in different ways these two occurrences which were born of such different intentions and produced such divergent results. On the other hand, they must recognize their common patriotic tone which for years was to form an integral part of the national tradition of struggle for independence.

In speaking of the Stanislavian period, the two uprisings on the one hand and the several-month-long war with Russia in 1792 on the other must be treated separately. The monarch, whose name was given to that era, was an opponent of the use of armed force in order to defend Polish independence. His was the policy of a wise but subservient man, a policy of compromise. Towards the end of his reign he was even prepared to sacrifice all just to retain his throne. And yet, Poniatowski's part in the reform movement, his contributions to rejuvenating the national economy and his patronage of the arts and learning in that period cannot be denied. He might even have gone down in history as the renovator of Saxon Poland, were it not for the external factors that accompanied the reforms initiated during his reign.

The Poland of Pulaski's and Kosciuszko's youth was marked by the transition from the Saxon to the Stanislavian period. Both their family histories were closely connected with the darkest days of the country. Ludwik Kosciuszko, Thaddeus's father, had held the rank of colonel in the Royal Army of Augustus III; this was an all but meaningless distinction, however, since at that time foreign armies were waging war on Polish soil. Nor could earlier generations of Kosciuszkos (who traced their ancestry to a Ruthenian named Konstanty — the diminutive of which was "Kostiuszko" — a courtier of Poland's King Sigismund I) boast of any more outstanding representatives of the military art.

The Pulaski family did have its knightly traditions, and Casimir's ancestors fought under King John Sobieski at Chocim and Vienna. His father, Józef Pulaski, was a lawyer by profession. He did hold membership in the Royal Hussars, although that was solely an honorary distinction. The public involvement of Thaddeus Kosciuszko's father did not go beyond the boundaries of his native county, and the title of swordbearer, to which he was entitled, had only symbolic significance. Casimir Pulaski's father by contrast sat in the

Seym from 1744 to 1754 and became widely known as an advocate of increasing the strength of Poland's army and reforming her monetary system. He enjoyed the reputation of a dynamic and skillful politician. At first he sided with the Czartoryski family which was opposed to the Saxon court; later he changed his allegiance and became a supporter of the Saxons. Owing to his political activity and his ability to make proper use of the support of influential patrons, Józef Pulaski gained a number of distinctions which, although lacking in actual significance, helped to advance his career in gentry circles. Aided by his protectors and his talent as a lawyer, he greatly increased his family estate. By the age of 60, as starost of Warka, he had amassed an impressive fortune. He owned 14 towns and 108 villages in various parts of the country (in the voivodships of Podlasie, Mazovia, Kalisz, Podolia, Volhynia and Bracław). To this might be added his wife's fortune, numerous starosties and other annuities.

Ludwik Kosciuszko did not attain wealth either as quickly or as easily. For many long years he leased estates in order to secure funds to regain possession of the family manor at Siechnowicze. That goal was achieved after his death by his widow, Tekla née Ratomska, the mother of Thaddeus.

Thus the childhood and adolescence of our two heroes unfolded quite differently, even though they were both of noble birth. These differences, however, were not limited solely to their families' financial situation. Thaddeus Kosciuszko was born on 4 February 1746 at Mereczowszczyzna in Polesie near the riverhead of the Narew, midway between Brest Litovsk and Novogrodek and lived in the provinces till the age of 19. Casimir Pulaski, born on 4 March 1747 at Winiary near Warka, some 60 kilometers from Poland's capital, as a child had frequently been in Warsaw with his father. Józef Pulaski, the starost of Warka, had a town house in Krakowskie Przedmieście. Nothing of his Warsaw residence has remained, but to this day one of the nearby streets bears the name of Warka (ulica Warecka). The Pulaski manorhouse at Warka—Winiary likewise is no more; although built towards the end of the 18th century, it stood for only slightly over a hundred years.

The Winiary estate had been a part of the dowry of Józef Pulaski's wife, Marianna Zielińska, the daughter of a wealthy gentry family, whom he married in 1736. The Pulaski family came from Podlasie. They were minor gentry from the vicinity of Biała Podlaska in the Białystok region. The name Pulaski derives from Pułaż, the family estate (hence the spelling "Pulaski" rather than "Pulawski", although the latter was also used occasionally).

Unlike the Pulaskis, the Kosciuszko family traced its ancestry to the eastern borderlands. The previously mentioned courtier Konstanty had received hereditary rights to the estate of Siechnowicze and a coat-of-arms from the king of Poland in 1509. His successors began using the name "Kosciuszko" and became rapidly Polonized. Seven generations later a son was born to the Kosciuszkos and christened Andrzej Tadeusz Bonawentura (although he himself would use only his second name). Thaddeus was the youngest of four children; his brother Józef was three years his senior and his two elder sisters were named Anna and Katarzyna.

He spent his childhood on his native hearth until the age of nine when he was sent to a school run by the Piarist Order at Lubieszów. The small wooden country house of the Kosciuszkos at Mereczowszczyzna has remained standing down to the present. The family estate of Siechnowicze was equally modest. Here Thaddeus stayed after leaving school at Lubieszów until 1765 when he left for Warsaw to join the Cadets' Corps. He also came to live at Siechnowicze 20 years later upon returning from America.

Not much is known about the first school attended by Thaddeus Kosciuszko. What is significant is that the 9-year-old Thaddeus and his then 12-year-old brother Józef were sent to the Piarist college rather than to the nearby Jesuit school. It was then that a reform in the spirit of the Enlightenment was getting underway in the schools operated by the Piarists under the supervision of Father Stanisław Konarski. It may be assumed that the school at Lubieszów was not bypassed by the new wave which, besides Latin, introduced the study of the Polish language, mathematics and the natural sciences and strove to train young people to be good citizens.

The Kosciuszko brothers spent five years at the Lubieszów college. The school's extant enrolment book indicates that in the school year 1759—60 Józef was enrolled in the highest class (rhetoric) and 14-year-old Thaddeus was in the second highest class (poetics). He did not complete his training, however, since presumably in connexion with the death of their father in 1758, the two brothers returned home to help their mother operate the estate at

Mereczowszczyzna and their subsequently recovered holdings at Siechnowi-cze. Thus, after some formal training, Kosciuszko spent most of his adolescence helping his mother with the task of running a country estate.

His later plans were considerably more ambitious, as at the end of 1765 he signed up for the newly created Knights' School in Warsaw, also known as the Cadets' Corps. His arrival in Warsaw marked a new chapter in the life of the then 19-year-old Thaddeus Kosciuszko.

Warsaw in the Stanislavian period was the center of Poland's intellectual life. It was receptive to new progressive trends and attracted many people from abroad (mainly France), radiating its influence across a still rather provincional and backward country. The beauty of Stanislavian Warsaw and the life of its streets were immortalized on canvas by the painter Bernardo Belotto-Canaletto. During the latter half of the 18th century the capital of Poland began developing at a most dynamic pace. In 1764 it had only 30,000 inhabitants, but within the three decades of Stanislaus Augustus' reign its population grew to some 100,000.

Casimir Pulaski, as has already been noted, became acquainted with the life of Warsaw at an early age. He became permanently associated with Warsaw after completing a parochial school (presumably at Warka) and enrolling in the school of the Theatine Fathers. A dozen years earlier this school had become well known for introducing the study of the natural sciences, but later suffered a decline in standards. At the age of 15 Casimir left this school which probably had not held much attraction for him; for he was able to acquire a great deal of knowledge and good manners by simply being in the bustling manorhouse of his father, the starost of Warka. He then became a page at the court of Prince Charles, the Duke of Courland and Semigallia (the southern parts of Livonia which remained fiefdoms of Poland till 1795), the son of the King of Poland, Augustus III. This court experience also provided the 16-year-old Casimir with his first taste of military life in 1763, when he spent six months in the camp of Prince Charles during the Russian siege of Jelgava, the capital of Courland.

The following year again found him in Warsaw in his father's charge. In September 1764 together with his father and brothers (Franciszek, two years his senior, and Antoni, five years his junior) Casimir participated in the election of Stanislaus Augustus Poniatowski. The election was a defeat for the Saxon faction to which Józef Pulaski had belonged. The latter was to become a foe of the newly elected monarch and later lead the armed forces of the anti-royalist Bar Confederation. As one of the leaders of the confederation, Casimir Pulaski too had nurtured the hope that his first patron, Prince Charles, would ascend the throne. The conflict between the Pulaski family and King Stanislaus Augustus would ultimately culminate in 1773 when the royal tribunal sentenced Casimir to death *in absentia* for his part in a confederate plot to abduct the monarch.

The relationship of the young Thaddeus Kosciuszko towards King Stanislaus Augustus was quite different from Pulaski's. As a member of the Cadets' Corps, a school of which the king was personal patron, Kosciuszko had direct contacts with the monarch on more than one occasion during his three and a half years of studies. He presumably gained the esteem not only of the commandant of the Cadets' Corps, Prince Adam K. Czartoryski, but also of the king himself, since he received a royal scholarship to supplement his studies in military engineering, as well as architecture, painting and drawing in France.

In the Cadets' Corps Kosciuszko had received a solid foundation in military engineering from outstanding lecturers brought to the new school from all parts of Western Europe by the founders of the first Polish military academy. After a year of studies, Kosciuszko received the rank of cadet and he spent the next two and a half years there as an instructor and also attended a special engineering course for particularly gifted students. In the fall of 1769 he traveled to Paris where he enrolled in the Académie Royale de Peinture et de Sculpture and also took private lessons from instructors in military science in accordance with the curriculum of the renowned École de Génie at Mézieres (as a foreigner he was not eligible for enrolment). Drawings made during his Paris sojourn attesting to Kosciuszko's artistic ability have been preserved. In the years that followed he would frequently return to drawing and sculpture.

Besides the secrets of military engineering and artistic skills, Kosciuszko also acquired during his stay in France political experience which was to prove invaluable later. His world view was moulded within the pre-revolutionary atmosphere of the philosophy and political thinking of the French Enlightenment. His nearly five year sojourn in France at a time of great impending change, when the first volumes of the renowned *Encyclopaedia* were appearing and Jean-Jacques Rousseau was calling for the equality and participation of the whole of society in the governing process, undoubtedly made an important imprint on the ideological education of the young Kosciuszko. These years marked the close of his youthful period.

The adolescence of Casimir Pulaski had ended several years earlier. He came of age at the same time he began his struggle in the ranks of the Bar Confederation. On 4 March 1768, his 21st birthday, he was named commander of one of the partisan detachments. It was at this point that the roads of Kosciuszko and Pulaski diverged most clearly. For while the former was enrolled at the royal military academy, the latter was beginning his fight against the principals of Stanislaus Augustus and his policies. Kosciuszko was faced by the prospect of several years of study in the course of which he would extend his military knowledge as well as his overall intellectual horizons. By contrast, Pulaski plunged into the thick of battle. Was he fully aware of its objectives, or was it his father's influence that induced him to take his place beneath the banners of the Confederation? Whatever the case may have been, at that point everything imaginable set the two young men apart. When Kosciuszko left the country during the second year of the civil war against the Confederation, he did so with a heavy heart. He had supported the Czartoryski camp, the adherents of the king. But did he view the Confederation solely as a band of trouble-makers? After all, his brother Józef had joined its ranks.

When Pulaski was forced to flee the country after the defeat of the Bar Confederates and found himself a wanderer in the Balkans, Kosciuszko was on his way back to Poland in 1774. But he soon found that for a graduate of the Cadets' Corps there was no career to be made in an army reduced in size in accordance with the partition treaty. His military education proved of little use, and the family estate of Siechnowicze, wallowing in debt due to his brother's mismanagement, was also unable to provide a livelihood. He thus availed himself of the hospitality of relatives and friends. He renewed his friendship with the household of Józef Sosnowski, began giving French lessons to his daughter Ludwika and soon intended to ask for her hand in marriage. But her father was opposed to such plans. Sosnowski, recently appointed hetman of Lithuania, reportedly told Kosciuszko: "Ring-doves are not meant for sparrows, and the daughters of magnates are not meant for minor gentry".

This blow was presumably what finally induced Kosciuszko to leave a country that had nothing to offer an officer with an all-round education. He decided therefore to seek opportunities for putting his skills to use elsewhere. In the fall of 1775 he returned to France, only to turn up a year later on the opposite side of the Atlantic, in Philadelphia. There, in the ranks of the American army, the 30-year-old Kosciuszko began his life as a man.

Stanislaus Augustus Poniatowski, the last king of Poland (1764—95), in coronation robes as portrayed by the court painter

The Polish magnates and gentry during the reign of King Stanislaus Augustus Poniatowski, as portrayed by Jean-Pierre Norblin: magnates ball; typical members of the gentry; a magnate and his henchmen

This is how the Warsaw of Pulaski's and Kosciuszko's youth (c. 1770) appeared to Canaletto, the author of a series of paintings devoted to Poland's capital.
Krakowskie Przedmieście — the main thoroughfare of 17th-century Warsaw: a view from the King Sigismund Column in Castle Square and a panorama of the street looking towards the monument

WIDOK WARSZAWY ZACZAWSZY OD PALACU SAPIEZYNSKIEGO   VUE DE VARSOVIE PRISE DEPUIS LE

Contrasts in 18th-century Poland: a panorama of Warsaw (after a painting by Canaletto in 1770) and rural scenes (sketched by Jean-Pierre Norblin)

Family portraits: Barbara and Ambroży Kosciuszko, Kosciuszko's paternal grandparents, and Tekla Kosciuszko née Ratomska, the mother of Thaddeus Kosciuszko (no portrait of Kosciuszko's father, Ludwik Tadeusz, has survived).
Baptismal certificate of Andrzej Tadeusz Bonawentura Kosciuszko, recorded in the parish register in the town of Kosów on 12 February 1746

Mereczowszczyzna, the birthplace of Thaddeus Kosciuszko (according to 19th-century illustrations and a photograph of the manor house after its restoration in 1926)

This is how Thaddeus Kosciuszko may have appeared as a boy; this hypothetical portrait was painted in the 19th century on the basis of pictures of the adult Kosciuszko (Kosciuszko's earliest posed portrait dates from 1792).

A page from the roster of pupils enrolled at the Piarist School at Lubieszów for the school year 1759—60; in a lower form (poetics) we see the 13-year-old Thaddeus, and in a higher one (rhetoric) is his brother, 16-year-old Józef.

The earliest extant signature of Kosciuszko was that found on a cash receipt, drawn up by his mother in 1764, and countersigned by both her sons. This document in effect closes the period of Kosciuszko's childhood spent at the family home in the Polesie region. A year later the 19-year-old Thaddeus Kosciuszko was to enroll in the Cadets' Corps in Warsaw.

A typical young Polish nobleman in Polish national attire, as depicted by Jean-Pierre Norblin. It may be assumed that both Kosciuszko and Pulaski dressed in this way in their early youth

View of the town of Warka, near which was located Winiary, the birthplace of Casimir Pulaski (after a 19th-century illustration); today Winiary is a suburb of Warka.

At the turn of the 18th and 19th centuries a house was erected in the old park at Warka-Winiary, where the Pulaski family home had once stood. It now houses the Pulaski Museum. In the park stands an obelisk erected by the townspeople in honor of Warka's most famous citizen

Józef Pulaski, starost of Warka, the father of Casimir Pulaski (after a portrait from c. 1750); there is no known portrait of Pulaski's mother and his original birth certificate has not been preserved

From early childhood Casimir Pulaski was exposed to the life of the capital, as Warsaw was only some 60 kilometers from Warka. At 13 he began studying in the school of the *Theatine Fathers;* the school building, which no longer exists, may be seen in this 18th-century *illustration (second from right).* Two years later, in 1762, Casimir became a page at the court of Prince Charles, the son of the then Polish monarch, King Augustus III of Saxony; Prince Charles and his wife Franciszka Krasińska, whose portraits are presented here, were to play an important role in Pulaski's later life. As a Bar confederate, he saw in Prince Charles the future king of Poland; tradition has it that Franciszka Krasińska was the only woman for whom Pulaski harbored great affection for any length of time

CAROLUS PR.PS REG. POLONIÆ

DUX. SAX. CURL. et SEMIG.

Ad vivum delineavit et in aere incidit Aug. de S.t Aubin Ill.mæ P.ssæ Caroli Curlandiæ Pinx Delineator et Chalcographus

On 6 September 1764 Stanislaus Augustus Poniatowski was elected king of Poland in Warsaw. The
event, in which the starost of Warka and his sons also participated, was committed to canvas by
Canaletto

nie ma z siebie wiadomości o sposobach ktoremiby oney
Ma z strony tych z ktoremi Daie pewne obowiązki
tczeli nie wypełni w dzieniu do szczegulowosci niepewnych trudności doyna.

Nauka wzięta Ktora pokazuie iako przyiść pirw-
sliwosci iako te przeszkody, ktore albo w nas się
strony tych z ktoremi żyiemy uchylone bydź nie
Ktora uczy nas iakich sposobow iuż toż z strony
iuż to z strony tych z ktoremi zostaiemy używać
iak iest potrzebna, iak iest potrzebny Srodek Sku-
osiągnienia kona

Część 4ta

1. Znaty potrzeby nauki wszystkie zgoła Narody
Narod Izraelski Ktoremu Salamon owe mąndrosci
piśy w Xięgach swych zostawił

2. Narod Chaldeyski ktory Prawidła sobie od Ludzi o-
rodne Dziatkom swoim wyraźnie wrażał

3. Egipyanie ktorzy zdania mąndrych Ludzi o Obyczaia
Jmillnem Tryznicista w ukrywosci y poszanowaniu

4. Persowie ktorzy synow Krolewskich y młodź siła
uczonym Panom swego Krolu porucali ktorych
wdle przepisu Zoroastra Boiaźn Jm Bogow y ro-
zny wrażał drugi do zamiłowania prawdy zachę-
sposobem zwyciężenia Namiętnosci własnych uczy
na czym mąstwo prawdziwe zawisło ukazywał

5. Grekowie ktorych Mędrcowie oni Sławni tak
tonowie Sokratesowie Arystotelesowie Xięgi Oby-
mądrych rad y zdań Pełne Oyczyznie iako drogi le-
podali

6. w Rzmie też nie zbywało na ludziach mądr oza
Dobra Rzpltego Znakomitych ktorzy potrzeb-
snaie przepisy oney iuż to w Rozmowach iuż to
szach pisanych y w mowach podali iako to o-
Jak Krolowie y Opalinscy Starowolscy Zipiy
Mądrzeiowy uczyli

Sta C.

Filozofia
Kościuszko
iam mam wyraw
wyraw Cci łaski, rowna
że łaielt moia rowinosc
Xiem wyraw w Łaszcze ile żyłte

In December 1765 Thaddeus Kosciuszko entered the Corps of Cadets in Warsaw. Although basically a military school, its curriculum went far beyond purely military matters. This is evidenced by a notebook containing Kosciuszko's notes and entitled "Philosophy".

The Corps of Cadets was accommodated in the Kazimierzowski Palace, now one of the buildings comprising Warsaw University

The mementoes left behind by Kosciuszko include sketches attesting to his artistic talent. All the reproductions presented here: "The Triumph of Flora", "Roman Ruins", "Portrait of a Man in Renaissance Dress", and the "Plan of Fort Czartorysk" are believed to have been executed during Thaddeus Kosciuszko's sojourn in Paris (1769—74). He had traveled to the French capital under a royal scholarship to supplement the knowledge acquired in the Corps of Cadets in the fields of military engineering, architecture and painting

80

Kosciuszko expressed his gratitude to Prince Adam K. Czartoryski, the commander of the Corps of Cadets, who personally arranged for the former's scholarship, by a drawing of an imaginary Fort Czartorysk with an allegorical scene showing a bust of Prince Czartoryski being decorated with a wreath of glory. The inscription on the monument reads: Gratitude in the heart is more lasting than bronze

After returning from a five-year sojourn abroad, the thoroughly trained officer-engineer was unable to obtain a commission. Also, his intention of marrying Ludwika Sosnowska came to naught owing to her father's opposition. The miniature, painted c. 1795 and thought to be a self-portrait, shows Kosciuszko much the way he must have appeared about the age of 30.

Beside it is a portrait of Princess Ludwika Lubomirska née Sosnowska, as well as sketches of the manor house at Sosnowica and the room in which Kosciuszko lived. When his matrimonial plans failed to materialize, Kosciuszko set off on his second foreign voyage, which led him across the ocean to fight under the standard of the American Revolution

83

A drawing by Thaddeus Kosciuszko entitled "Poland"

Chapter III

Casimir Pulaski as a Member of the Bar Confederation

On 29 February 1768 at the town of Bar, in the south-east corner of Poland not far from the Turkish frontier, an armed organization of the gentry known as the Bar Confederation was formed. Its establishment came about at a time when in Warsaw the Seym, under pressure from Catherine II's ambassador, was adopting legislation contrary to Poland's interests as a state. This concerned issues which during the first three years of Stanislaus Augustus's reign had caused bitter political struggle between the king's supporters (i.e. advocates of reforms aimed at strengthening state authority) and their conservative adversaries opposed to any restrictions on the "golden freedom" of the nobility. Stanislaus Augustus, whose candidacy to the throne had been supported by Russia in 1764, from the very outset displayed great initiative and energy in promulgating legislation to strengthen the government. This, however, was not to the liking of Tsarist Russia which was opposed to the excessive independence of the Polish ruler. To an even greater extent it was disturbing to the Prussians who would have preferred to see anarchy prevail in Poland.

In order to weaken the two factions and set them at loggerheads with each other, Russia and Prussia hatched a plot centering on the issue of extending rights to religious minorities in Poland (Orthodox and Protestant Christians), equal to those enjoyed by Catholics. The king, backed by a group of progressive political figures, sought to eliminate manifestations of religious intolerance, in order to improve relations in this domain, as well. But the overwhelming majority of magnates and conservative gentry, traditionally tied to Catholicism, were violently opposed to such measures. On 27 June 1767 a confederation was established at Radom under the slogan: "In Defense of Faith and Freedom". One of its organizers was the starost of Warka, Józef Pulaski. The Radom confederates sought to depose Stanislaus Augustus whom they considered a despot and an opponent of the gentry's liberties. In their political naïveté they deluded themselves into believing that through Russian assistance they would succeed in placing the Saxon pretender on the Polish throne, thereby restoring "the Saxon era". The Russian ambassador Repnin played the role of mediator. In the Seym, which came to be known as "Repnin's parliament", in an atmosphere of terror and intimidation he forced through resolutions which satisfied neither of the feuding factions and constituted an overt attempt at imposing alien designs on the Poles. The ability of the gentry to dissolve parliament was restricted although not eliminated in principle, and partial rights were granted to members of religious minorities. Certain of the laws enacted during the first three years of Stanislaus Augustus's reign remained in force, but the possibility of further reforms was curtailed. The principles of Poland's policy were legislatively proclaimed "eternal and immutable", and their inviolability was to be guaranteed by the Russian Tsarina. This constituted a formal limitation of Poland's sovereignty, though the pretence that this had occurred at the will of the Seym was maintained.

Józef Pulaski had not participated in that session of parliament. After a personal run-in with Repnin, he left Warsaw and, without even consulting the main leaders of the anti-royalist faction, he began making preparations for armed resistance. His determination and belief in the necessity of armed struggle attested to the mood that swept many Polish patriots who began to doubt in the effectiveness of legal political action.

The starost was no young fire-brand. And yet, this prosperous 64-year-old squire, skillful lawyer and experienced politician plunged the country into civil war in a hasty, politically immature and militarily ill-prepared manner. The founders of the Bar Confederation had counted on the assistance of Turkey, France and Austria, which were interested in weakening Russo-Prussian influence, but they failed to secure such support. Militarily the Bar Confederates had counted on the spontaneous participation of the gentry in a movement whose slogans appealed to religious sentiments and proclaimed gentry freedom. But it was probably the atmosphere of religious warfare flaring up in the confederate camp which explained the lack of foresight and poor preparation of the venture. The chief agitator at Bar was Father Marek Jandołowicz, an inspired preacher. The confederates chose as their patron Our Lady of Częstochowa whose image was emblazoned on their banners. The confederation's inner circle adopted the name Order of the Knights of the Holy Cross, and had as their motto "Jesus-Mary". The political aims that permeated this undertaking can be briefly summed up as follows: overthrow the despotism of the king and Tsarist Russia; through the aid of foreign allies elevate Prince Charles of Saxony to the Polish throne; restore a gentry commonwealth cemented by the common love of "golden freedom" and a common Catholic faith; and protect the homeland from the designs of reformers. The distinguished specialist in 18th century Polish history, Professor Emanuel Ros-tworowski, has written: "Conservative, religious and patriotic motives were so closely interwoven within the Barist ideology, that it is difficult to ascertain whether the confederation was more of a 'counter-revolution', a religious war or an independence movement".

After several months of unsuccessful skirmishes with Tsarist and Polish royal forces in Podolia and the Ukraine, the founders of the confederation fled to Turkey following the fall of Bar (20 June 1768). At the outset of the following year the nucleus of the insurrectionist movement moved to Little Poland, and at the end of 1769 a new political and military leadership sprung up in Silesia (at Biała) called the General Council of Confederated Estates, known in short as the Generalty. But, whereas the Barist period was characterized by selflessness and fanatical religious elation, in later years there was a visible increase of in-fighting among the various magnate coteries, aimed at securing private influence and benefits after the overthrow of Stanislaus Augustus. On the other hand, as the movement grew and its ranks were swelled by an increasing number of burghers and peasants, it lost the markings of "a gentry war". It also ceased to be " a religious war", with people of various religious persuasions reinforcing its troops and leadership. In the heat of battle various social groups began to rally round the overriding issue: independence. But that issue turned out to be a lost cause. Following the defeat of the confederation, the first partition of Poland was carried out. The armed resistance of the Poles served to speed up the decision of the neighboring powers, caused their views on Polish affairs to converge and led to the most drastic of measures — the annexation of a part of Poland's territory.

The problem of achieving a final and complete assessment of the influence exerted by the Confederation on Poland's later destiny has remained to the present a controversial one. All historians agree, however, that it marked the first instance of the nation's determination to fight in defense of its existence in the 100 years since the war against Sweden in the mid-17th century, and that it played an important role in the later struggle for independence.

Among the heroes of the confederate struggle Casimir Pulaski has occupied the leading place. It was he who personified all that was best in the movement: a love of freedom and an unshakeable faith in the victory of those who struggle against despotism. He was to be guided by the same ideals in his struggle for American independence. As a commander Pulaski displayed enormous initiative and was independent to the point of licence. He was the personification of verve and audacity, combined with endurance and relentlessness. He sought no personal gain, spared no effort and constantly risked life and limb in the course of his four and a half years of military service. In one of his letters from that period he wrote: "... I will allow nothing in this world to separate me from my sincere intentions towards the Homeland. I expect no benefit other than death for the honor of God and the Homeland, which, surrounded by hazards, it becomes me to await in impeccable virtue."

Pulaski served as commander in over a dozen major confederate actions and numerous skirmishes. He frequently lost, but he always succeeded in rallying his men again for the fray. His campaigns took him the length and breadth of Poland, from Podolia to the Poznań region and from Silesia to Lithuania*. He became famous as the defender of the Jasna Góra fortress at Częstochowa. Prior to that he had defended Berdyczów and the Holy Trinity Trenches, but he was at his best on an open battlefield. He mainly commanded mounted detachments assisted by infantry, and he went in for mobile partisan actions based on lightning-swift maneuvers and the unexpected switching of forces into new positions. The extraordinary energy, courage and dash of Casimir Pulaski aroused respect and fear in the enemy. The commanders of the Tsarist corps pitted against the confederates considered him the most relentless of adversaries and the most difficult to defeat.

The leadership of the Confederation displayed mixed feelings towards the capable, though at times self-willed partisan. Internal friction and factional intrigues within the Generalty cut Pulaski off from broader participation in the general command, although attempts were made to make him commander-in-chief and dictator. He himself made no efforts in this direction. His element was combat, not strategy. He was a nobleman in whose veins there flowed the blood of those who had once fought under the banners of King John Sobieski. He was guided by a soldier's instinct rather than by cold calculation.

The military career of Casimir Pulaski began on 4 March 1768, four days

---

* See map on page 103

after the proclamation of the Bar Confederation. Józef Pulaski headed the military organization, and his son Casimir was named commander of a troop. Within several weeks his troop numbered some 1,000 men. All told, the Confederation had a strength of 5,000 men, when word arrived that a Tsarist expeditionary force, which had been formed at Repnin's urging to quell the uprising, was advancing from Volhynia. Royal Polish troops had also been sent to Podolia for the same purpose.

At the end of April 1768, two months after the Confederation had been formed, Casimir Pulaski got his first taste of battle when he defended Stary Konstantynów against a Russian attack. Suspecting that the bulk of confederate forces had been concentrated there, the Russians moved on to the east towards Chmielnik. Pulaski, at the head of several hundred confederates, followed in pursuit. In a marshy area near Kaczanówka he found himself in an ambush and sustained considerable losses; nonetheless, he managed to make his way to Chmielnik which he defended from a Tsarist onslaught.

In mid-May Pulaski moved to Winnica in the vicinity of which he engaged in several skirmishes with the enemy. Subsequently he occupied the fortified monastery at Berdyczów so as to provide support to the north-easternmost area of confederate military operations, namely Żytomierz. There preparations were underway to proclaim the confederation's expansion into Kiev voivodship. Pulaski's troop strength at Berdyczów amounted to 1,400, whereas the Russians besieging the monastery numbered some 5,000. The Tsarist forces began an artillery bombardment of the monastery, but its fortified walls provided protection to the defenders. But their cannons soon fell silent one after another for lack of ammunition, and the confederates' supply of food and water began to dwindle. On 13 June, after a siege lasting more than a fortnight, the monastery was forced to surrender. Pulaski and his garrison were taken captive by the Russians. A week later Bar, the cradle of the confederation, also fell. The remaining some 2,000 confederates, including Casimir Pulaski's father and two brothers, crossed the Dniester and took refuge on Turkish territory near Chocim. There they were joined by Casimir who was released after a month's captivity. The first chapter of the confederates' struggle had come to a close, its most eventful pages written in the thick of combat by Casimir Pulaski.

Now began a period of guerrilla warfare in the Dniester river area. Casimir Pulaski made raids on the northern bank of the river to conduct reconnaissance and secure provisions. On 6 October the Turkish sultan declared war on Russia. The hearts of the confederates were filled with new hope, but among the leaders who took refuge beyond the Dniester with their troops feuding and intrigues flared up. As a result, Józef Pulaski was arrested by the Turks. The young Pulaski brothers broke away from the remainder of the inactive confederate forces and captured the Holy Trinity Trenches (Okopy Św. Trójcy) and Żwaniec forts on the Polish side of the Dniester. From the Holy Trinity Trenches Casimir Pulaski made it as far as Zaleszczyki and Tłuste, where he engaged in skirmishes with Tsarist forces sent to fortify the Turkish frontier. For that purpose a Russian expeditionary corps consisting of 4,000 men had been despatched to the scene in early March. The troops commanded by the Pulaski brothers numbered only about 1,000. They could not count on Turkish assistance, since the Turks had not taken any steps against the Russians, despite their declaration of war. What is more, on the eve of the confrontation Antoni, the youngest of the Pulaski brothers, was captured by the Russians.

On 8 March 1769 a sudden attack was launched on both the castles simultaneously, so as to prevent them from aiding one another. Despite bitter resistance Żwaniec was the first to fall. Franciszek Pulaski then retreated to the southern bank of the Dniester. The fate of the Holy Trinity Trenches, defended by Casimir Pulaski, was sealed by a nocturnal siege. When the last fortifications fell, Pulaski together with 200 men fled through a secret passageway which led through the rocky escarpment to the river-bank. After a skirmish with the Russian cavalry, they made their way across the swollen Dniester to the Turkish side. Franciszek Pulaski and his company sought refuge with a friendly pasha at Chocim. Casimir Pulaski bypassed the fortress and moved on towards the River Prut, thus ending his second confederate campaign. At that time Józef Pulaski died in Turkish captivity, but word of the heroic exploits of his sons had undoubtedly reached the starost of Warka before then.

The third chapter in Casimir Pulaski's career as a Bar confederate began with his company's 400-kilometer march from Bukowina, where he had sought refuge after retreating from the Holy Trinity Trenches, to Little Poland.

After passing Czerniowce, he approached the Polish frontier which he crossed near Kute. Making his way along the northern slopes of Czarnohora and Gorgany, he found himself towards the end of March near the Łupków mountain pass. The aim of that march was to establish liaison with the confederates of Little Poland who had continued the insurrection initiated at Bar. The latter, however, were more involved in internal feuding than in armed struggle. Thus the moment Pulaski learnt that a company led by his brother had arisen in eastern Little Poland, he hastened to join forces with it. Their meeting took place in mid-May at Sambor. The brothers resolved to operate in unison without seeking outside support and derived their marshal's mandate from the gentry of the Przemyśl region which was then in the process of forming a confederation " in the image and likeness of the act of the Bar Confederation ". Franciszek, the elder of the two brothers, was named marshal of the Przemyśl region.

The first joint venture of the Pulaski brothers was to be the capture of Lvov. Their forces were extremely limited, but they were joined by Józef Bierzyński, one of the more accomplished commanders of Little Poland. The siege proved unsuccessful. Disconcerted by the approach of Tsarist units, the confederates retreated from Lvov and split up their forces. That move was taken advantage of by the Russian commander Drewitz, one of the harshest suppressors of the insurrectionist movement, who had already boasted of crushing confederate unions in the regions of Poznań, Sieradz and Wieluń. He first attacked Bierzyński's forces, inflicting heavy losses. The companies under the command of Casimir Pulaski fared somewhat better in their encounter with a part of Drewitz's army at Krystjampol. That marked the first encounter between two commanders who were to meet in battle with varying results on more than one occasion.

After disengaging from battle, the forces of the Pulaski brothers and Bierzyński moved up into the Lublin region in order to set up a new leadership in an area hitherto unencompassed by confederate operations. Bierzyński pushed ahead of the Pulaskis, incorporating under his banners units of private magnate armies (at Zamość) and companies of pro-confederate noblemen (at Puławy). The Pulaski brothers left the Lublin region under Bierzyński's command and moved on through Polesie up into Lithuania. In July Confederations were established through their inspiration at Brest, Volkovysk, Slonim and Grodno. The political side of these undertakings was directed by Franciszek Pulaski, while Casimir concentrated on the military aspect. This stirring up of trouble in Lithuania forced the Russians to transfer troops thither from Great Poland. Drewitz was sent up to Lithuania from the south and an expeditionary force was also despatched from Vilna, but Casimir Pulaski succeeded in routing the latter on 6 July at Kukielki. A week later at Slonim he came off best in an encounter with reinforcements which had been sent from Great Poland. But Casimir Pulaski avoided a major frontal encounter with Drewitz, preferring to withdraw into the virgin forests of Augustów where his forces were able to set ambushes and win several skirmishes.

The Pulaskis were forced to retreat, however, before the enemy succeeded in deploying a larger concentration of forces. The trail of the confederates led through Szczuczyn and Łomża on towards Drohiczyn. Casimir Pulaski stopped along the way at Ostrołęka where a confederate gathering named him marshal of the Łomża region.

The Pulaskis then marched on towards Brest and Kobryń, but were encircled by four columns of Tsarist forces. On 13 September at Orzechów they put up a battle. In their retreat through the forest marshes under pressure from the Russian infantry the confederates were unable to deploy their artillery. When they finally succeeded in taking defensive positions and began their artillery barrage, Russian cavalry units attacked from the rear, forcing them to change front. Ultimately the decimated Polish units managed to reach the River Bug, but when they found themselves on the opposite bank there too they encountered Russian forces. Avoiding an encounter, they retreated in the direction of Włodawa, but there they were met by a fresh column of Russian soldiers. Panic broke out among the Poles as a result of this unexpected turn of events. Casimir Pulaski rallied some of his more valiant comrades in an attempt to check the enemy advance. Once apprised of what had occurred, Franciszek Pulaski, who had withdrawn from Włodawa earlier, returned with his men to relieve Casimir's force and help to organize their retreat. But once again their retreat was blocked by the enemy, and the oldest of the Pulaski brothers was killed by a bullet in the ensuing battle. After 500 Poles had fallen in that encounter — including his brother who was

his closest comrade-in-arms — Casimir Pulaski and the remaining Polish survivors fled in total disarray. Such was the tragic finale of the Pulaski brothers'
four-month campaign, which had begun with their meeting at Sambor and
concluded in defeat and the death of one of them at Włodawa.

Ten days later, on 23 September 1769, Casimir Pulaski turned up at
Zborov in Slovakia, on the territory of the Austrian Empire which extended
asylum to confederate refugees. Pulaski spent the fall of 1769 and the winter
of 1770 in the Carpathians near the river-head of the Wisłoka, recruiting
and training an army for new combat missions. He also carried out guerrilla
raids and was seriously wounded in the arm during a skirmish at Grab.
He constantly awaited the opportunity to avenge the disastrous Lithuanian
campaign, but his stroke of bad luck seemed to endure. A bold raid by
1,200 cavalrymen in the direction of Tarnów ended in defeat at Pilzno (15 May
1770).

The following armed action also failed to bring Pulaski fame. This was
the Battle of Wysowa, waged on 3-4 August against Tsarist forces concentrated at Podgórze. The mountainous terrain was ideally suited to irregular
hit-and-run warfare, but the Generalty and Pulaski himself had their sights
set on greater successes. In the event of an unfavorable turn in the battle
the confederates counted on retreating into Austria which in fact they did.
But the pursuing forces of Drewitz also crossed the frontier, outflanked the
Poles and inflicted serious losses upon them. Once again Drewitz had got
the upper hand of Pulaski.

The ill-fated Battle of Wysowa did, however, mark the beginning of
Casimir Pulaski's proudest period in the service of the confederation. The
zenith of his triumphs was his defense of Częstochowa. Several weeks after
the Battle of Wysowa, Pulaski sent his infantry units into the more tranquil
environs of Biała, while he himself led the cavalry in pursuit of Drewitz's
forces which had moved from Podgórze to the north-west. On the night of
1 September he carried out a raid on Cracow, capturing the barracks in a
surprise attack and placing 250 cavalrymen from the royal garrison under
his command. With these reinforcements he swiftly withdrew from Cracow
the same night. Several days later near Pińczów he encountered some of
Drewitz's units which had marched into the area upon learning of the attempt

to capture Cracow. Pulaski did not engage Drewitz in any major encounters but succeeded in eluding him by taking his troops on a wild goose chase throughout the Polish countryside. Ultimately he outwitted his adversary, for when the latter attempted to block Pulaski's approach to Radom and Warsaw, the Polish commander turned up at Częstochowa. On 9 September 1770 he captured the fortified monastery and placed its garrison under his command. From that time up till the end of the insurrection, the monastery at Jasna Góra would remain in confederate hands.

The monastery at Jasna Góra gained the reputation of an impregnable fortress in 1655 when it was unsuccessfully besieged by the invading Swedes. The capture of the monastery by Pulaski was therefore a feat of both strategic and moral significance. Moreover, this national shrine with its miraculous picture of the Black Madonna of Częstochowa had always had special meaning for Poles.

In the fall of 1770 Pulaski carried out raids from his base at Częstochowa in the direction of Żarnowiec and Jędrzejów, establishing liaison with confederates from the Poznań region and leading his forces to the gates of Poznań itself. In the meantime, Drewitz was preparing to capture Częstochowa and on New Year's Eve he began his siege of the monastery. He had 3,000 men under his command, supported by his own artillery as well as pieces borrowed from the Prussians. The Polish forces under Pulaski numbered 500 cavalry and 800 infantry. One-half of the fortress' 150 cannon were prepared for battle. Upon construction of firing embankments the Russian artillery began its bombardment with 30-kilogram cannonballs, but they proved incapable of breaking down the thick walls of the monastery. Meanwhile, Pulaski organized raids beyond the monastery's walls, destroying Russian artillery pieces and decimating their crews. After several days Drewitz directed an all-out siege under cover of darkness, but that also proved futile. The artillery atop Jasna Góra inflicted heavy losses on the attackers whose ladders, moreover, were too short to scale the walls. After unsuccessful attempts Drewitz called off his siege. All of Poland rejoiced, including royalist opponents of the Confederation who did not conceal their satisfaction at the humiliation suffered by the Tsarist forces. Memories of Częstochowa's proud tradition during the Swedish invasion were reawakened. Pulaski was now popularly referred to as "the defender of Częstochowa", and foreign newspapers provided extensive coverage to his feat.

Częstochowa now became Pulaski's base for both small-scale actions and more ambitious raids. The biggest such undertaking was the attempt to create a "second Częstochowa" from the fortified town of Zamość. Pulaski began this campaign in May 1771, marching towards the Lublin region from Podgórze via Tymbark, Limanowa, Nowy Sącz and Dębica towards Zamość (with skirmishes along the way at Kolbuszowa, Dębica and Mielec). This undertaking was contrary to the plan of concentrating forces at Lanckorona, drawn up by Dumouriez, the French military adviser of the Generalty, and demonstrated Pulaski's disregard for the confederate leadership. The raid did succeed in drawing Russian forces away from the Polish units stationed at Podgórze, but Pulaski was unable to capture Zamość which was held by Polish forces loyal to the king. When an attempt at negotiation also proved unsuccessful, Pulaski — ever faithful to the principle of avoiding fratricidal bloodshed — withdrew without a fight. Fleeing from pursuing Russian forces, he returned to Częstochowa just in time to prevent Polish loyalist troops from capturing the monastery in his absence.

In October 1771 Pulaski undertook one last major expedition. This time he marched at the head of his army in the direction of Warsaw as part of a confederate plot to abduct King Stanislaus Augustus. Pulaski's detachment was to receive the captive and put him in a safe place, perhaps at Częstochowa. The actual abduction was organized by a nobleman from Lithuania, one Stanisław Strawiński, who had consulted with Pulaski on this matter earlier. The entire plot misfired, however. Late in the evening on 3 November the plotters did succeed in abducting the king from his carriage as he rode to supper, but they subsequently dispersed for fear of being pursued. As a result, the king found himself escorted by a sole abductor, whom he ultimately induced to set him free with promises of an amnesty and reward. The same night Stanislaus Augustus was back in his castle. The part of the plot, which Pulaski's detachment was to have carried out, also failed. On its way to Warsaw it came upon Tsarist forces at Skaryszew near Radom and engaged them in a skirmish. The confederate detachment was routed and Pulaski, who had sustained an arm wound, fled the battlefield on a borrowed horse together with the remaining survivors in the direction of Częstochowa. The odium of hatching a plot against the king himself fell upon Pulaski. In fact he was accused of being the principal instigator of the scheme, especially when the Generalty denied all involvement in it in order to save face. The epilogue to this affair took place in September 1773 in Warsaw when the royal tribunal accused "the infamous Pulaski" of complicity in attempted regicide and sentenced him to death *in absentia*. It was only 20 years later (14 years after Pulaski's death) that this sentence was abrogated by an act of the Seym.

The final episode of Pulaski's participation in the dwindling struggle of the confederation continued to center round Częstochowa. The monastery still attracted survivors from routed confederate units. But when Russia and Prussia concluded a treaty concerning the partition of part of Poland's territory (17 February 1772), and were subsequently joined by Austria, Pulaski saw the futility of further struggle. He reckoned with the possibility of the imminent encirclement of Jasna Góra which would lead either to a last-ditch stand or to capitulation, neither of which would have benefited anyone. With the indictment for "regicide" hanging over him, Pulaski could not run the risk of being captured. So as not to allow his personal affairs to complicate the situation for the entire garrison, he decided to leave Częstochowa. He bade farewell to his faithful comrades-in-arms and crossed over into Prussia. The most renowned partisan of the Bar Confederation had left his homeland, never to return. His dedication to Poland would one day be recalled by historians, but before that time, he was also destined to become a New World hero at Savannah.

One of the three best-known 19th-century portraits of Casimir Pulaski (cf. the reproductions on pp. 15 and 20)

Br. Zaleski ad. f.

Casimir Pulawski Confoederations Marschall.

Joh. Martin Will excudit Aug. Vind.

18th-century German copperplate portraying Casimir Pulaski as one of the marshals of the Bar Confederation; the inscription in German and Latin speaks of the heroism of those who fight for the freedom of their homeland

MANIFESTE
DU
COMTE
DE
PULAWSKI

Maréchal de Lomza &c. &c.

Ma vie me fut chere tant que je pus l'employer au service & à la défense de ma patrie. Je ne m'arreterai pas à donner des preuves de ce sentiment qui a dirigé toute ma conduite; je ne pourrois les rapporter sans faire mon éloge, & par conséquent, sans être taxé de vanité & d'amour-propre. Je me contenterai donc de dire que j'ai pour témoins irréprochables de ma conduite, & les citoyens vertueux qui ont défendu la même cause que moi, & nos ennemis mêmes qui m'ont vû combattre avec

tous les termes qui auroient pû déplaire à la seule Jurisdiction que j'ai reconnuë, avec la plus grande partie de ma nation. Je proteste contre tout pouvoir illégal & usurpé de la *Confédération actuelle*, & contre tous les actes qu'elle a pû faire, & principalement contre le Decret qu'elle a si injustement porté contre ma personne. Je proteste que l'action détestable qu'on m'a calomnieusement imputé, ne m'est jamais venuë dans l'esprit. Tout ce qu'on peut me reprocher c'est, d'avoir servi ma patrie, avec tout le zèle & toute la force dont je suis capable. Je ne saurois me disculper de ce reproche; & si c'est là un crime, j'avoue que je suis & que je veux mourir coupable. Donné à Francfort, le 5. Octobre 1773.

(signé)
PULAWSKI.

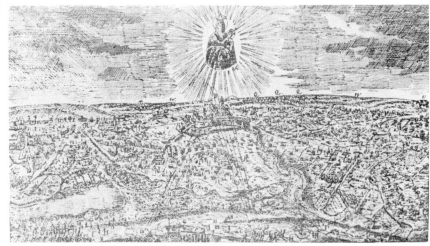

During the Confederation's four years of struggle (1768—72) an important role was played by fortified points of resistance held by individual insurrectionist detachments. The defense of Berdyczów is depicted by an 18th-century illustration. In June 1768, after a two-week-long engagement with Russian forces, Casimir Pulaski was forced to retreat. A week later tsarist troops captured Bar, the birthplace of the Confederation. A 19th-century lithograph shows the remnants of the fortified walls at Bar

Chocim, a well-known Podolian fortress on the southern bank of the Dniester, was under Turkish occupation in the 18th century. Its walls (whose might was still visible on this early-20th-century photograph) could thus provide refuge to the survivors of the routed insurrectionist units. Here Józef Pulaski sought refuge after the fall of Bar, and the brothers Casimir and Franciszek Pulaski retreated in this direction after the loss of the Żwaniec and Holy Trinity forts situated on the northern bank of the Dniester

Casimir Pulaski amongst the leaders of the Bar Confederation (a page from The Album of the Bar Confederation, published in 1899)

BITWY I POTYCZKI KAZIMIERZA PUŁASKIEGO
(1768 – 1772)
BATTLES AND SKIRMISHES IN WHICH
CASIMIR PULASKI TOOK PART (1768–72)

granice Polski przed I rozbiorem (1772)
Poland's Frontiers before the First Partition (1772)

103

Casimir Pulaski after a 19th-century miniature. Right: portion of an exhibition in the Pulaski Museum at Warka (display case containing medallions, weapons and other mementoes of the Bar Confederation)

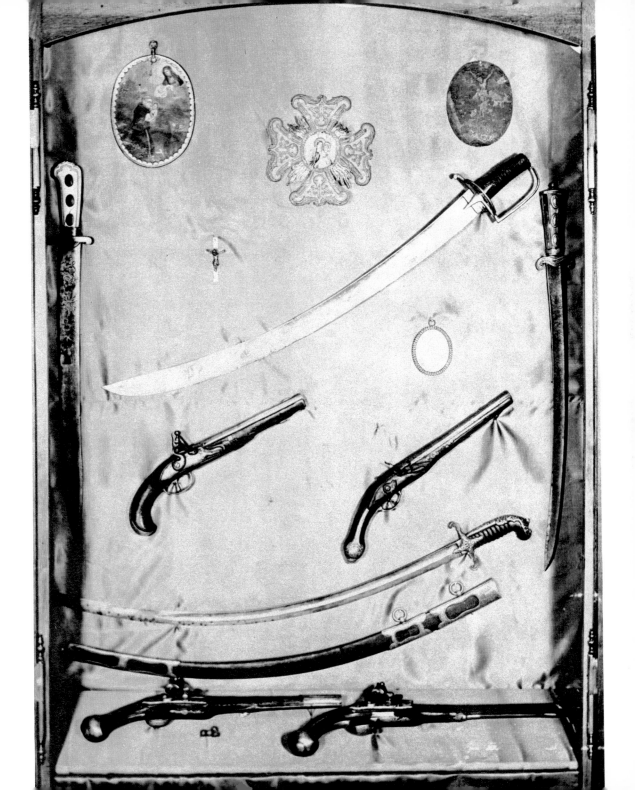

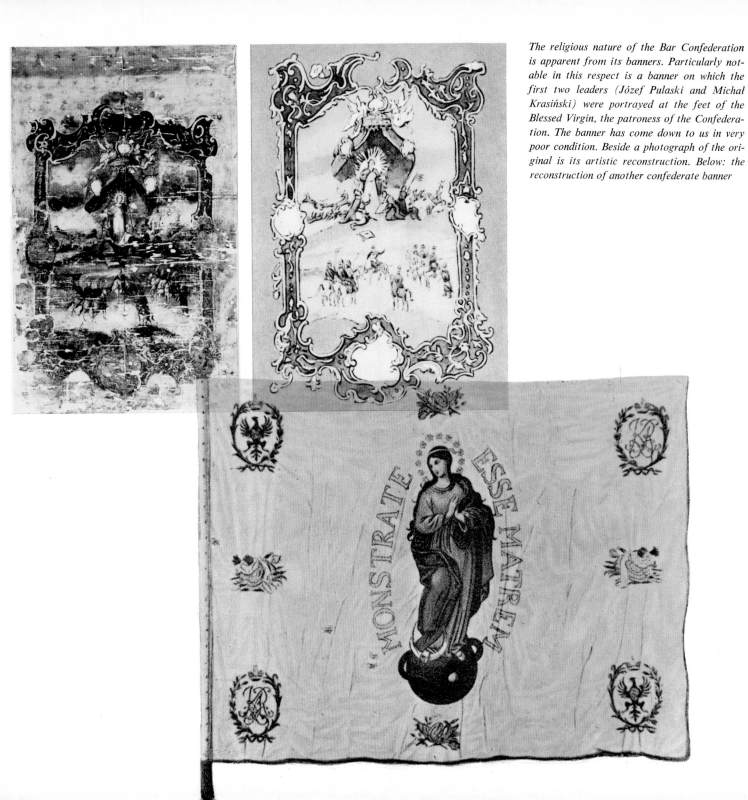

The religious nature of the Bar Confederation is apparent from its banners. Particularly notable in this respect is a banner on which the first two leaders (Józef Pulaski and Michał Krasiński) were portrayed at the feet of the Blessed Virgin, the patroness of the Confederation. The banner has come down to us in very poor condition. Beside a photograph of the original is its artistic reconstruction. Below: the reconstruction of another confederate banner

MONSTRATE ESSE MATREM

Two fairly well-preserved ornamental plates of the Confederation in gilded copper (photos show both sides of the plates)

Uniforms worn by some of the Bar Confederation's cavalry and infantry units

The Bar Confederation was a rather infrequent topic of 19th-century painting. The prayer of the confederates prior to the Battle of Lanckorona was painted by Artur Grottger, and Józef Brandt committed one of the Confederation's skirmishes to canvas

Earlier than either of the above-mentioned paintings is a work by Kornel Szlegel. It appeared during the first half of the 19th century and portrayed one of Pulaski's adventures during his struggle along the river San near Słomno. It seems that Pulaski had been invited to a manor house for a christening. He accepted the invitation and arrived in the company of a single comrade-in-arms. During the feast the manor house was surrounded by a Cossack detachment, but Pulaski and a comrade were said to have held off the enemy onslaught with their swords until relief from the Polish camp arrived

An incident which received a great deal of publicity at home and abroad was the confederate attempt to abduct the King of Poland. The action, carried out in Warsaw on 3 November 1771, ended in failure. King Stanislaus Augustus Poniatowski, who was abducted from his carriage late one evening and taken out of town, succeeded in convincing one of the conspirators to release him. Casimir Pulaski, who had not taken part in the attempted abduction, was charged with instigating the conspiracy and was sentenced to death in absentia by a royal tribunal. The attempt to abduct the king in order to compel him to cooperate with the Bar Confederation was termed the "attempted regicide". The incident became the talk of Europe. In Germany there appeared a series of illustrations portraying the attempted abduction of the Polish monarch. One of them depicted in successively numbered scenes the entire course of the incident

"Casimir Pulaski at Częstochowa" (painted by Józef Chełmoński in 1875). The defender of Jasna Góra is shown at the head of charging cavalry making a sortie from the fortified citadel which he captured on 9 September 1770, defended in January 1771 against an attack by tsarist forces aided by Prussian artillery, and held on to till the end of the confederate war. From here he organized raids in the direction of Poznań, Warsaw, the Lublin region, Cracow and the Carpathian Foothills. He left Częstochowa on 31 May 1772 and made his way abroad

The Paulite monastery atop Jasna Góra in Częstochowa (after a watercolor from the early 19th century)

The treasury of the Jasna Góra Monastery to this day contains the Cross of Pulaski, a decoration presented to him on 2 February 1771, after his successful repulsion of the siege of the monastery. The motto inscribed on the cross: "Pro Fide et Maria, pro Lege et Patria" (For the Faith and Mary, for the Law and the Fatherland) differs from that of the royal Order of the White Eagle: "Pro Fide, Lege et Rege" (For Faith, Law and King). Pulaski reportedly made a votive offering of his cross to Our Lady of Częstochowa, the patroness of the Bar Confederation. The decoration is the most valuable authentic memento left behind by the hero of the confederate struggle, as it attests to the fact that the leadership of the Confederation considered his defense of Częstochowa to be an act of exceptional merit

The highly abbreviated and vague Latin inscription on the arms of the cross is difficult to decipher. Expanded, those abbreviations read: BENE MERENTI IN CLARO MONTE DIE 2 FEBRUARII 1771 CASIMIRO PULASKI MARESCHALKO LOMZENSIS TRIBUTUM PRAEMIUM (Awarded to Casimir Pulaski, Marshal of Łomża, on 2 February 1771 in recognition of his merit at Jasna Góra)

Przyjaciel Ludu.

ROK SIODMY.   No. 38.   Leszno, dnia 20. Marca 1841.

Kazimierz Puławski.

Dyaryusz oblężenia Częstochowy w roku 1770.

(Ciąg dalszy.)

Dnia 7. Stycznia. Dzień z rana przepędzony bez attaku. O godzinie 9., gdy jazda nieprzyjacielska w kilkadziesiąt koni po domach około Ś. Rocha rozgrzaniem się bawiła, dobre strzelanie armatne od fortecy odległych nie raziło. Wtém porucznik od infanteryi łomżyńskiéj, za ordynansem Puławskiego wysłany, kominami, na pogorzelisku stojącemi, ku kościołowi Ś. Rocha przeszedłszy, żołnierzy i koni kozackich znacznie ranił i kilkunastu Kozaków z końmi komenderowanymi zabił. A gdy piechota nieprzyjacielska od Ś. Rocha wyszedłszy, sukursować swoich chciała, on piechotę aż na cmentarz zapędził, i domy stojące zapalić kazał. Wtém dwa szwadrony karabinierów i mnóstwo Kozaków, z pod Ś. Barbary przypadłszy, od fortecy oderwać go chcieli; a ten od Ś. Rocha posilony sukursem, nieprzyjaciela brać i natarczywie

118

Somewhat different from the most commonly encountered images of Casimir Pulaski was a portrait painted in the latter half of the 19th century, probably on the basis of an earlier miniature (cf. reproduction on p. 104)

KAZIMIERZ PUŁASKI

A monument to Casimir Pulaski by Xawery Dunikowski commissioned for the Polish pavilion at the New York World's Fair in 1939

120

Chapter IV

Kosciuszko and Pulaski in the Struggle for US Independence

The conflict between the thirteen British colonies in America and the motherland had been growing over a period of many years. It became visibly aggravated in 1763 when Great Britain considerably expanded and consolidated her hold on America at the expense of France and Spain. From then on Britain would begin the increasingly brutal economic exploitation of her American possessions. Various forms of economic pressure (additional taxation, increased customs tariffs etc.) together with the repression of those who refused to submit thereto only served to consolidate the American colonists in opposition to the motherland. The inhabitants of the thirteen colonies, each of which constituted a separate administrative unit, began to acknowledge a growing community of interests. King George III of England and British parliament displayed an uncompromising attitude towards attempts at slackening the colonies' ties of absolute dependence, although originally the colonists' demands had been limited to the most modest repesentation in the British parliament. There had been no talk of full independence or of severing ties with Great Britain to which the American colonists were closely bound and which they considered to be their common homeland. But when the British proved unable or unwilling to reach an understanding, preferring to introduce various forms of pressure, and when the British army began to liquidate the munitions stores, meant for the American militia for use in self-defense, bloodshed proved inevitable.

On 19 April 1775 at Lexington and Concord in the colony of Massachusetts the first armed encounter between American units and British troops took place. The latter had been despatched from Boston for the purpose of destroying the military storage depots of the American colonists. At Lexington, along the way to Concord, the conflict claimed its first victims. The same day the British were attacked, both at Concord and during their return march, by the colonists. All told, 95 Americans and 173 British soldiers lost their lives that day. A state of war broke out between Massachusetts and Great Britain and soon engulfed the remaining 12 colonies. Although nobody realized it at the time, that incident marked the beginning of the American War of Independence.

Three weeks after the events at Lexington and Concord the Continental Congress convened at Philadelphia. As the representative body of the thirteen (originally twelve) colonies, it took upon itself the duties of a national government representing the interests of all Americans. The membership of the Congress included Benjamin Franklin and Thomas Jefferson, the latter one of the more republican minded of the American leaders. On 15 June 1775 the Congress appointed George Washington commander-in-chief of the Continental Army.

A petition sent to George III by the Congress contained assurances of the Americans' desire to maintain links with the motherland on condition that their grievances be recognized but it was rejected by the king, who issued a proclamation calling for the necessity of "quelling the rebellion and mutiny". War between the colonies and the homeland became inevitable, the more so as further skirmishes with British troops had taken place since those of Lexington and Concord. Under the circumstances the notion of proclaiming total independence began to gain in popularity.

The act referred to as "The Unanimous Declaration of the Thirteen United States of America" was adopted by the Continental Congress on 4 July 1776. The essence of this document was the contention that "these United Colonies are, and of right ought to be, free and independent states, that they are absolved from all allegiance to the British Crown, and that all political connection between them and the state of Great Britain is, and ought to be, totally dissolved."

The US Declaration of Independence, whose principal author had been Thomas Jefferson, became the cornerstone of the new state and its polity It was written in the spirit of the social doctrines of the Enlightenment. For many years to come it would remain a document of the aspiration towards national liberation and towards the creation of such a form of government as would ensure all citizens of full rights. In that period the republican United States, the first independent state in the Western Hemisphere, became a symbol of the struggle for national and personal liberty to all to whom the Old World seemed too cramped and backward, too despotic and unjust. The Declaration of Independence, the basic document of American history, made use of the name "United States of America" for the first time. The substance of the declaration also exerted influence on the aspirations for independence of other nations.

The Declaration reads in part as follows:

"We hold these truths to be self-evident, that all Men are created equal, that they are endowed by their Creator with certain unalienable Rights, that among these are Life, Liberty, and the pursuit of Happiness. — That to secure these Rights, Governments are instituted among Men, deriving their just powers from the consent of the governed, — That whenever any Form of Government becomes destructive of these Ends, it is the Right of the People to alter or to abolish it, and to institute new Government, laying its foundation on such principles and organizing its powers in such form, as to them shall seem most likely to effect their Safety and Happiness."

When the Continental Congress was adopting the Declaration of Independence in Philadelphia, Thaddeus Kosciuszko was already on his way to America, and Casimir Pulaski was making every effort to receive permission to go there from the American delegate in Paris. It would appear, therefore, that earlier news of the struggle gaining impetus across the Atlantic must have caught the attention of the two Poles. When he left Poland in the fall of 1776 Kosciuszko may have already known about the initial armed encounters between the Americans and British and he may have heard about the appointment of Washington as commander-in-chief. But in all likelihood it was not until after his arrival in France that he decided to travel to America. That decision was undoubtedly influenced by the atmosphere of great interest and sympathy displayed by the French towards the colonies attempting to shake off the yoke of British despotism. After the recent loss of its American possessions to Britain, France at first became a natural ally of the Americans. In a semi-legal fashion the French extended financial assistance, supplied food and clothing and also aided in recruiting volunteers. Among one of the first groups of recruits was Thaddeus Kosciuszko. His qualifications in fortifications engineering were particularly useful to an army composed mainly of people with but a scant knowledge of military affairs.

The commander-in-chief of the American army was faced with many difficulties. Recruitment was proceeding less smoothly than anticipated and the enlisted men under his command lacked training and discipline. Equipment, uniforms and food were in short supply. Throughout the war Washington was plagued by these problems and it was only his strong will, perseverance and authority that enabled him to organize an army and instill in it the will to fight. It should be remembered that the war with the British Crown did not enjoy much popularity among the bulk of colonists, who were accustomed to the old situation and wary of republican innovations. American farmers and craftsmen were by and large unwilling to abandon their farmsteads or work- shops for any length of time. They were prepared to take part in battle but not to serve in the regular army. Under the circumstances educated military specialists like Thaddeus Kosciuszko and battle-tested commanders like Casi- mir Pulaski were worth their weight in gold to Washington.

But Pulaski's efforts to set sail for America were to drag on for many long months. Perhaps his past (the accusation of attempted regicide) and the fact that his name was well known to the courts of Europe had been among the reasons that permission was not granted him sooner. To Pulaski, whose sole vocation had been military service, enlistment in Washington's army meant an opportunity to serve a cause befitting a champion of freedom. The five years that had elapsed since his departure from Poland were a time of exile and wandering. After the fall of the Bar Confederation he spent nearly two years in Germany and France, and then moved on to the Balkans to fight the Russians at the side of the Turkish army. Shortly thereafter, however, Turkey was defeated and concluded a peace treaty with Russia. Pulaski again turned up in France. When his attempt to gain assurances of safe conduct back to Poland proved futile, in the summer of 1776 he commenced efforts to travel to America. In May of 1777 he received a letter of recommendation from the United States commissioner in France, Benjamin Franklin, and on 23 July of that year he landed at Marblehead near Boston. In August he reported to Washington's headquarters near Philadelphia.

Thaddeus Kosciuszko had arrived in America a year earlier, most likely in late July or August of 1776 (the exact date is unknown). After landing in Philadelphia, then the seat of the Continental Congress, he offered his services to the Board of War*. Before receiving the official nomination of engineer with the rank of colonel in the American army on 18 October, he was told to design fortifications on the Delaware River. Their purpose was to protect

---

See map on page 140

124

Philadelphia from a possible attack by the British fleet which at any moment could have sailed into the mouth of the river and posed a threat to the town. Kosciuszko designed a system of fortifications which were to be situated at Billingsport, three miles downstream from Philadelphia. He envisaged rows of palisades driven into the riverbed as a deterrent to landing, defended by an artillery redoubt on the bank overlooking the river. This initial design demonstrated the engineering skills which Kosciuszko had acquired during his studies in Paris. He must have appeared exceptionally capable, moreover, since he generally managed to compete successfully against the similarly educated Frenchmen serving in the American army. Kosciuszko worked on his fortification scheme at Billingsport and Red Bank on the Delaware until April 1777. During that time he was befriended by his superior, General Horatio Gates, and when the latter was appointed commander of the northern army, Kosciuszko followed him to New England, near the Canadian frontier. In view of the threat of a British invasion from the north he was ordered to study the possibility of reinforcing the defenses of the frontier fortress of Ticonderoga on Lake Champlain. After becoming acquainted with the local topography, Kosciuszko concluded that a nearby 15-meter-tall elevation known as Sugar Loaf Hill would be the ideal site for a battery of cannons whose long range would provide effective protection to the fortress. The undertaking was approved by General Gates. At this juncture, however, change in command occurred, and the new chief of the northern army made light of the issue, restricting the Polish military engineer to tasks on the fortress grounds. The faultiness of that appraisal became apparent when the British approached Ticonderoga, moved their artillery into place atop the Sugar Loaf Hill and thus compelled the American army to abandon the fortress. In the course of a prolonged retreat Kosciuszko, as chief engineer of the northern army, distinguished himself by the initiative which he showed in fortifying successive camps and retarding the British pursuit through the construction of various obstacles.

When General Gates was put in charge of the northern army anew, Kosciuszko's role increased considerably. The commander had him choose the best site for stationing the army in anticipation of a decisive confrontation with the British. Kosciuszko selected a hilly area overlooking the Hudson

River near Saratoga, known as Bemis' Heights, which he fortified with a five-kilometer-long earthwork. In September and August of 1777 this was to be the scene of bitter fighting culminating in the capitulation of the British army. The Battle of Saratoga ranked among the major victories achieved by the American forces and was largely decisive for the further course of the war. After that battle France officially recognized the independence of the United States and openly sided with the Americans in their war against the British. After Saratoga Thaddeus Kosciuszko won considerable recognition, since the victorious commander, General Gates, publicly acknowledged his role in that successful encounter. The American commander-in-chief, General George Washington, also became aware of Kosciuszko and six months later gave him the important assignment of fortifying the fortress of West Point on the Hudson. Its purpose was to protect the waterway linking the northern and southern parts of the United States against the British.

Kosciuszko spent two-and-a-half years designing and supervising the construction of fortifications at West Point which was to mark his greatest engineering achievement. The fortress at West Point comprised a polygonal citadel, situated atop a rocky escarpment 60 meters above the river, and four forts, three of which were sited on neighboring hills. The fourth, situated on the riverbank, was meant to defend a ship barrier in the form of an impregnable chain with two-foot-long links which was strung across the river. In addition, there were seven redoubts strategically situated between the forts. The fortress was to be manned by a garrison of 2,500 soldiers. As in other instances, here once again Kosciuszko succeeded in making optimal use of existing physical features for fortification purposes. For years his creation was to remain the biggest American fortress. In 1802 West Point became the site of America's renowned military academy, and in the early 19th century a monument commemorating its builder was erected there.

For a while West Point served as George Washington's headquarters. He had been interested in building the fortress earlier, and during an inspection tour of the fortifications being built by Kosciuszko in mid-1778 he met the Polish engineer, presumably for the first time. Besides official expressions of approval, there are no records to indicate any special acknowledgement on Washington's part for Kosciuszko's efforts, neither in the form of the promotion he so richly deserved after Saratoga nor even a letter of commendation of the type which the commander-in-chief generously lavished on his subordinates. The correspondence between Washington and Kosciuszko was always cool in tone. This reserve may be accounted for by Kosciuszko's intimate relationship with Gates, an antagonist of the commander-in-chief. Noteworthy is Washington's letter written to Congress after the Battle of Saratoga, in which he referred to Kosciuszko as "a gentleman of science and merit" who very much deserved to be remembered. Kosciuszko was known to be ambitious though modest — not the type of person to strive after personal gain. As a result, his achievements were not recalled until after the war.

After West Point, the next stage in Kosciuszko's American career was his involvement in the partisan battles of the southern army, to which he was assigned in August of 1780. There new experiences awaited him. As the chief engineer of a relatively small formation (consisting of several thousand men) engaged in a highly mobile style of combat, he organized numerous crossings of a river that cut across the battle area and carried out engineering projects during the siege of Fort Ninety-Six. As a front-line commander, he also led his soldiers into battle. Kosciuszko's two-and-a-half-year stint in the southern army provided much valuable combat experience which would later prove useful to him as a divisional commander in the Polish-Russian war of 1792 and subsequently as commander-in chief of the insurrection of 1794.

In the final phase of the American War of Independence Kosciuszko participated in the siege of Charleston, South Carolina, the last town defended by the British even after parliament had declared an end to the war and the initiation of peace negotiations. During the operation he again served both as a fortifications expert and a front-line commander. On 14 December 1782 Kosciuszko triumphantly rode into Charleston at the head of General Greene's units, thus ending his six and a half year military career in the service of the United States.

For a year-and-a-half after the war had ended, until July 1784 when he set sail from New York for Europe, Kosciuszko remained in America. It was only then (13 October 1783) that Congress promoted him to the rank of general. An even greater expression of recognition was the admission of Kosciuszko, as one of three foreigners, into the Society of the Cincinnati, an organization affiliating the most outstanding veterans of the American War of Independence. It was named after the ancient Roman leader considered to personify the ideal civic virtues of the soldier farmer. Among the duties of the society's members was "to contribute to the promotion of freedom among people". Kosciuszko was to remain faithful to that ideal throughout his life.

Thaddeus Kosciuszko's sojourn in America lasted eight years, of which more than six were taken up by the war. This was twice as long as Casimir Pulaski's period in American service. Little more than two years were to elapse between his first battle on 11 September 1777 and his death from wounds received during the battle of Savannah on 11 October 1779*.

"I came here, where Freedom is being defended, to serve it, and to live or die for it," wrote Pulaski in his first letter to George Washington, in which he offered his military services to the American cause. If Pulaski had encountered difficulties in receiving permission to travel to America, it must be admitted that once he arrived he was given a most cordial reception. Washington recommended Pulaski to Congress, as a result of which he was appointed general of the cavalry on 15 September 1777. Prior to that he had taken part in the Battle of Brandywine Creek in which Washington's forces suffered a defeat. But the counterattacks carried out by Pulaski provided cover for the retreating Americans and helped to prevent a military disaster. Thus, even before he officially became a soldier in the American army, Pulaski had demonstrated to the commander-in-chief the battle skills of a bold cavalryman, rapid in maneuver. Soon thereafter he took part in the Battle of Germantown (4 October 1777), where Washington was again defeated and his cavalry units, divided into small groups, were unable to play a major role.

Pulaski's appointment as general of the cavalry meant his taking command of all the mounted units in Washington's army. However, this amounted to a very modest force consisting of several hundred cavalrymen scattered throughout the army and attached to infantry brigades mainly for the purpose of carrying out reconnaissance missions. As the organizer of the American cavalry, Pulaski's entire effort would be aimed at turning these mounted units

* See map on page 158

into a more effective and independent combat force. Within a year he had under his command four regiments of light dragoons totaling 700 men.

Pulaski spent the winter of 1777 together with his cavalry at Trenton, in the vicinity of Valley Forge where Washington's army was stationed under extremely dire conditions. Despite countless difficulties and shortages, Pulaski did not let up in his efforts to perfect the combat training of his soldiers. He introduced new battle drills in an effort to transform the heavy dragoons into highly mobile uhlans armed with lances — weapons hitherto unused by the American army. As a commander he was extremely demanding and his relations were none too cordial with certain American officers who complained of his exceedingly high requirements. For his part, Pulaski complained in his letters to Washington of a lack of understanding for his initiatives.

In the spring Pulaski's dragoons took part in a campaign to rid New Jersey of British troops. The action was directed by General Anthony Wayne to whom Pulaski's cavalry was subordinated. But the conflict of ambitions that ensued ultimately prompted Pulaski to tender his resignation. Washington agreed, seeing that the independent-minded, mettlesome Polish partisan was out of his element in a post that required the coordination of every action with others. And although the American commander himself represented an entirely different cast of mind, he retained full confidence in Pulaski and continued to regard him with affection.

Pulaski's request to be relieved was connected with the earlier intention of creating under his command a special infantry and cavalry unit capable of more independent action. Washington supported this venture in Congress which on 28 March 1778 consented to the formation of the Pulaski Legion consisting of 68 cavalrymen and 200 foot-soldiers. The legion came into being in Baltimore, Maryland, where, towards the end of April, he set up his headquarters. Pulaski now displayed a new-found vitality and enthusiasm as he devoted all his energy and his private funds as well towards this undertaking. It took five months to form the legion. It was composed of representatives of various nationalities: Americans, Frenchmen, Poles, Irishmen and Germans, the latter (mainly deserters from Hessian mercenary units fighting in the British army) being the most numerous.

In May the legion's banner was officially dedicated and in August Pulaski reported that his unit was ready for action and requested his first combat mission. Neither Washington nor Congress, however, had any clear-cut notion of how the new formation might be deployed. It was only after much persistent petitioning by Pulaski that he was ordered into the vicinity of Egg Harbor in New Jersey to protect the coast against an expected British assault by sea. Unfortunately, as a result of the desertion of several soldiers who went over to the enemy side, the British launched a night raid and surprised the sleeping legionaries. Thirty members of the legion lost their lives, and the incident put a damper on the unit's combat activities for some time. Perhaps, as a result of the desertions at Egg Harbor, it was decided to isolate the Pulaski Legion from direct contacts with the British. It was sent into a remote northern area bordering on lands inhabited by Indians, against whom a punitive expedition was being prepared. A mission of that type did not meet the ambitions of Pulaski, however, who again tendered his resignation, requesting at the same time that the Legion be deployed in a different theater.

On 2 February 1779 it was decided that the Pulaski Legion be sent to South Carolina to reinforce the army of General Benjamin Lincoln, the commander in the southern states where armed encounters with the British had flared up recently. Pulaski led his detachment out of the north to Yorktown, increased their troop strength to 600 and headed south towards Charleston. Thus began the most active period of Pulaski's American service. At long last the legion found itself in front-line combat. Upon arriving in Charleston on 8 May it defended the town against the British who, having occupied the state of Georgia and having captured Savannah, were now invading South Carolina. Pulaski organized a number of forays out of Charleston which was encircled by the British, and although the legion suffered seriou, losses, the enemy was forced to retreat.

At the turn of May and June 1779 Pulaski was engaged in observings British troop movements and carried out a number of guerrilla raids and reconnaissance missions. In this kind of partisan warfare he was in his element. But with the advent of the hot season, all activities subsided. The Pulaski Legion was stationed at that time at Augusta (cavalry) and Sheldon (infantry). Pulaski himself frequently traveled to Charleston.

The third fall in his American career, which was to be marked by his final act of heroism at the Battle of Savannah, was rapidly approaching. The plan to capture that town called for the joint efforts of the Americans and French troops under Admiral Charles Henri d'Estaing which had only just landed in America. Pulaski, whose legion had been stationed near Savannah since mid-September, was among the first to greet the French allies.

An all-out assault on the heavily fortified town entailed great risk. But the French admiral, concerned about the threat to his ships posed by the British, refused to wait until saps were dug, as it would take a week before they reached the British redoubts. Under these circumstances, it was decided to begin the siege on 9 October.

Savannah was surrounded to the east, south and west by a ring of 13 fortresses. The town's northern flank bordered on the river. A marshy area formed its western foreground. The attack was to be spearheaded by French units attacking one of the redoubts on the south-west side. At the same time other detachments were to feign an assault from the east and south, whilst several frigates were to sail up the river towards the town and thereby harass the British rear. The mission of the Pulaski Legion was to follow in behind the French infantry, penetrate the area among the individual redoubts and break down the enemy's line of defense. This intricate plan to confuse the enemy with feigned attacks, followed by a massed assault on a preselected redoubt, failed. The units which were to feign an attack from the east became bogged down in rice-fields. The attack, which was to have been launched before dawn, did not get underway on schedule, and in the daylight the Americans became easy targets for British cannon and musket fire. To make things worse, the British had been apprised of the main line of attack the previous day by an American deserter.

As a result, when the French infantry, led by Admiral d'Estaing, lunged for the abatis encircling the British redoubts in the morning sunlight, they found themselves in a crossfire. Still, it appeared that the combat-seasoned French foot-soldiers, supported by American infantry, would succeed in penetrating via a narrow path through the marshes. The first assault columns were already atop the enemy earthworks when they were countered by crack Scottish infantry assigned to defend the most threatened of the British redoubts. Under heavy grape-shot fire d'Estaing thrice attempted to reassemble his infantry in the narrow marshy pass for successive attacks, but was ultimately wounded.

The Pulaski Legion was awaiting the proper moment for the cavalry to enter the scene, but that moment did not arrive. From afar Pulaski could see the infantry breaking ranks under heavy fire. It was then he decided to launch one final assault amid the retreating infantrymen. Leaving his legion beyond a hill, in the company of only his adjutant, Captain Bentalou, Pulaski charged the Springhill redoubt where the fiercest battle was raging. There he was felled by a round of grapeshot.

The seriously wounded Polish commander was bleeding profusely as he was carried from the battlefield. A surgeon removed the walnut-sized bullet which had lodged in his groin. Pulaski was in critical condition. He was taken in a co a to the brig *Wasp* which was to transport him to Charleston by sea. On 11 October Pulaski died without regaining consciousness. Since the extreme heat made it impossible to ship his remains to Charleston, he was buried at sea, reportedly near the place where the Savannah River flows into the Atlantic.

Thus ended the biography of the 32-year-old Casimir Pulaski, Bar confederate and general in the American republican army, defender of the independence of Poland and of the United States.

The Order of the Cincinnati, established in 1783 after the victorious termination of the US War of Independence. The order was the insignia of the society of the Cincinnati to whom the most outstanding participants in the war belonged. Thaddeus Kosciuszko was one of three foreigners to receive this decoration for his more than six years of service to the cause of American freedom, before he returned to his homeland to devote himself to restoring its independence.

The photograph shows a copy of the old medal: an eagle, the emblem of the USA, on a blue, white-bordered ribbon; the eagle's breast bears a likeness of the order's patron, the Roman dictator Lucius Quinctius Cincinnatus (5th century B.C.) who, upon fulfillment of his military duty towards his homeland, returned to till the soil. The motto of the order was: "Omnia relinquit servare Rempublicam" (He forsook all to save the Republic)

Drawn by Earl & engraved by A.Doolittle in 1775   Re-Engraved by A.Doolittle and J.W.Barber in 1832

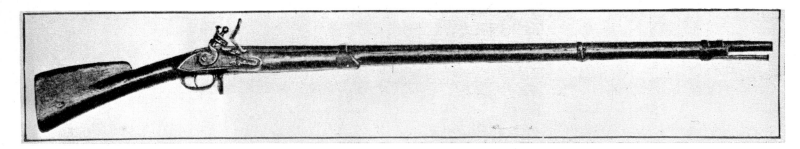

A skirmish at Lexington (near Boston) on 19 April 1775 between a 70-strong American militia detachment and a British unit, despatched from Boston to Concord in order to confiscate an arms cache of the American patriots. That minor skirmish was to give rise to the war for American independence. The museum at Lexington to this day displays one of the muskets used by American patriots in that memorable battle

The first major armed encounter with the British was the Battle of Bunker Hill at Charlestown (near Boston) which took place on 17 June 1775. The ill-trained but spirited American troops succeeded in repulsing the attack of the British regulars; this 18th-century illustration portrays one of the attacks on the American positions (left side of drawing)

Facsimile of the original manuscript of the US Declaration of Independence drawn up by Thomas Jefferson, with corrections introduced by Benjamin Franklin and John Adams. Beside it: a facsimile of the final text of "The Unanimous Declaration of the Thirteen United States of America" adopted by Congress on 4 July 1776

Thomas Jefferson (1743—1826)
Benjamin Franklin (1706—90)
John Adams (1735—1826)

Independence Hall in Philadelphia, where Congress ratified the Declaration of Independence

The commander-in-chief of the American Revolutionary Army surrounded by high-ranking commanders who came from Europe to fight for the American cause. Standing left to right: George Washington, Johann de Kalb, Frederick William von Steuben, Casimir Pulaski, Thaddeus Kosciuszko, Maria Joseph de Lafayette and John Peter Mühlenberg. This 19th-century German illustration bears the symbolic title "Council of Generals at Valley Forge", for the personages portrayed never were there together. Pulaski indeed met Washington when he was on patrol service in the vicinity of Valley Forge in the winter of 1777, whilst Kosciuszko's first meeting with Washington probably took place at West Point no earlier than 1778.

The camp at Valley Forge, near British-occupied Philadelphia served as the winter quarters for Washington's army in 1777—78. Conditions of great hardship prevailed: primitive quarters, hunger, a lack of suitable winter clothing and a smallpox epidemic. As a result, only 4,000 troops of the original 11,000-strong army were combat ready come spring. Three thousand soldiers had died. It was only Washington's energy and authority that prevented the total disintegration of the army. In the photo: a present-day view of the environs of Valley Forge with cannon dating from the Revolutionary War in the foreground

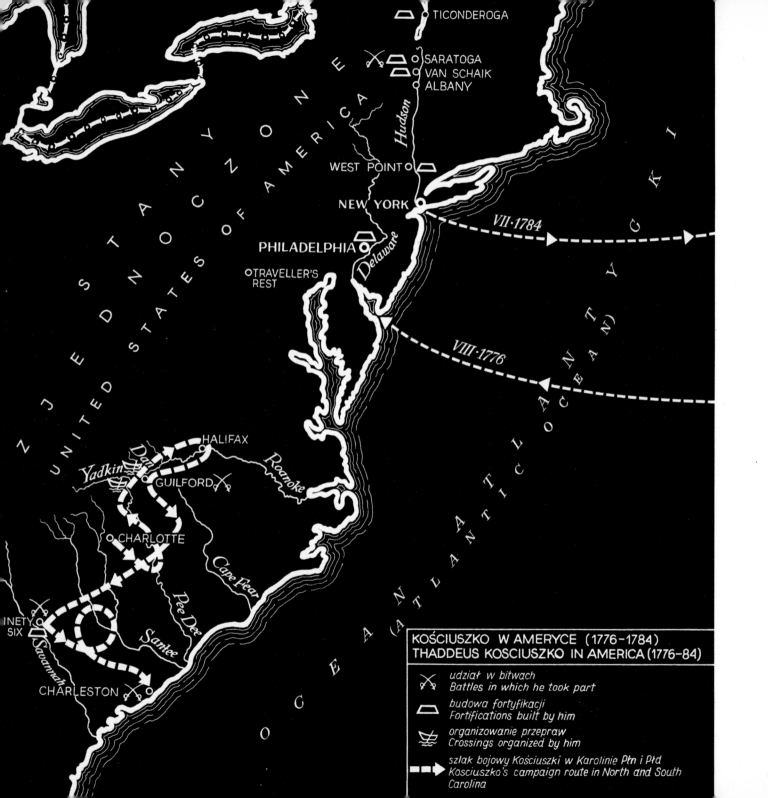

TICONDEROGA

SARATOGA
VAN SCHAIK
ALBANY

Hudson

WEST POINT

NEW YORK

PHILADELPHIA

Delaware

TRAVELLER'S
REST

VII·1784

VIII·1776

HALIFAX

Yadkin

Dan

GUILFORD

Roanoke

CHARLOTTE

Cape Fear

Pee Dee

INETY
SIX

Santee

Savannah

CHARLESTON

Z J E D N O C Z O N E

U N I T E D   S T A T E S   O F   A M E R I C A

S T A N Y

O C E A N   (A T L A N T I C)   A T L A N T Y C K I

O C E A N

KOŚCIUSZKO W AMERYCE (1776–1784)
THADDEUS KOSCIUSZKO IN AMERICA (1776–84)

⚔ udział w bitwach
Battles in which he took part

⏢ budowa fortyfikacji
Fortifications built by him

⛴ organizowanie przepraw
Crossings organized by him

⟶ szlak bojowy Kościuszki w Karolinie Płn i Płd
Kosciuszko's campaign route in North and South
Carolina

140

This 19th-century color lithograph of Kosciuszko In America is fairly well-known. This imaginary portrait does capture some of his facial features, but the attire depicted lacks authenticity. The telescope and the riverbank in the background seem to indicate the author's intention of emphasizing Kosciuszko's achievements in fortifying West Point overlooking the Hudson River

THE COURSE OF
DELAWARE RIVER
from PHILADELPHIA to CHESTER,
exhibiting the several WORKS erected by the REBELS to defend its Passage,
with the ATTACKS made upon them by His MAJESTY's Land & Sea Forces.

Engraved by William Faden Charing Cross, April 30, 1778.

PHILADELPHIA

P E N S Y L V A N I A   S H O R E

Kingsefs Creek

Province Island

Carpenters Island

Bow Creek

Hog Island

Fort Island

Mud Island

Red Bank Island

Billings Island

Billings Point or Billingsport

Coopers Point

Mantto Creek

New Redoubt

T H E   J E R S E Y   S H O R E

Two Miles.

142

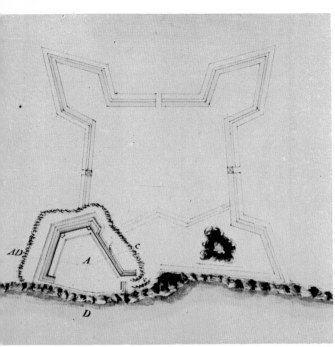

Map of fortifications along the Delaware River (downstream from Philadelphia) which were to defend the building of Congress from British warships approaching from the river's mouth. The design and subsequent construction of the fortifications at Billingsport and Red Bank were the work of Thaddeus Kosciuszko from October 1776, soon after his arrival in America, till April 1777. The map reproduced here was drawn up in 1778; Billingsport is visible at bottom left. A fort was erected on the riverbank (see adjacent plan), and several rows of piles were driven into the riverbed. Incidentally, these fortifications failed in autumn 1777 to protect Philadelphia from the British who captured the town by land.

A set of six etchings depicting 18th-century American towns. The first shows Philadelphia seen from the Delaware

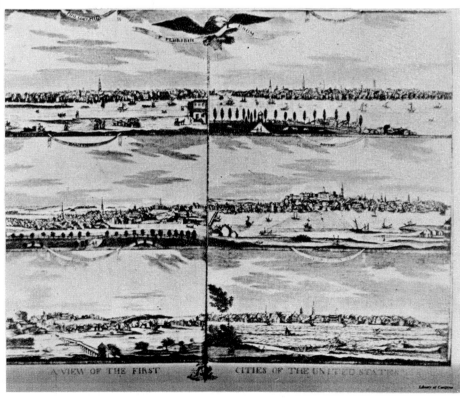

A VIEW OF THE FIRST   CITIES OF THE UNITED STATES

143

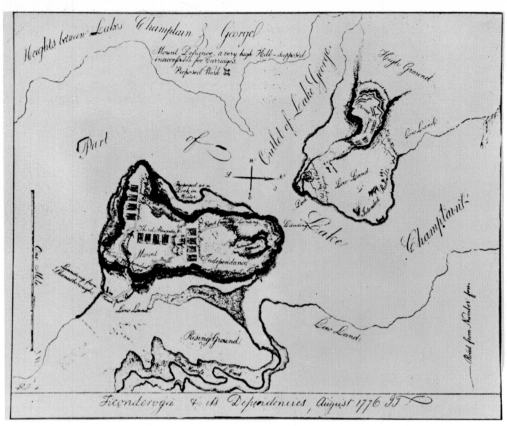

During the northern campaign in spring 1777, Thaddeus Kosciuszko was ordered to assess the defense potential of Fort Ticonderoga on Lake Champlain, marking the US frontier with Canada, whence a British attack seemed imminent. The map of this vicinity, drawn up in 1776, shows Mount Defiance (top), also known as Sugar Loaf Hill, where Kosciuszko had intended to locate a battery to defend Fort Ticonderoga. His concept was never implemented, and as a result the fort fell to the British and the Northern Army, in which Kosciuszko served as chief engineer, was forced to retreat.

A view of Ticonderoga as presented by an 18th-century illustration. Next to it, a present-day view of the historic fort

144

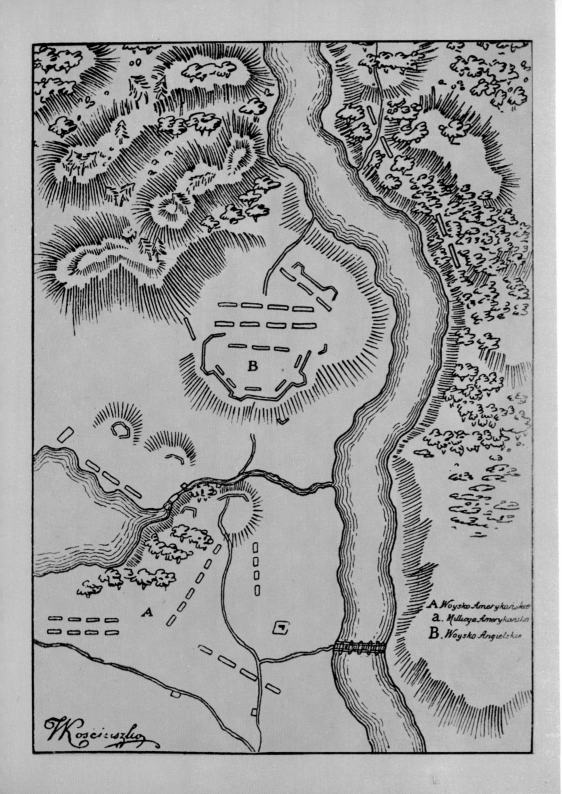

A Woysko Amerykanskie
a. Millicya Amerykanska
B. Woysko Angielskie

T.Kosciuszko

On 17 October 1777 at Saratoga the Northern Army forced a 7,000-strong British corps to capitulate, marking the first American victory of the Revolutionary War. The commander of the Northern Army, Gen. Horatio Gates, gave much of the credit for that victory to Thaddeus Kosciuszko, his chief engineer, the designer of field fortifications. The plan outlining the distribution of troops and fortifications at Saratoga, drawn up by Kosciuszko, is now a valuable document attesting to his contribution to the American victory.

Right: the Battle of Saratoga according to a 19th-century lithograph; below: facsimile of the closing part of the British act of capitulation, signed on the American side by Gen. Gates and on the British side by Gen. Burgoyne

146

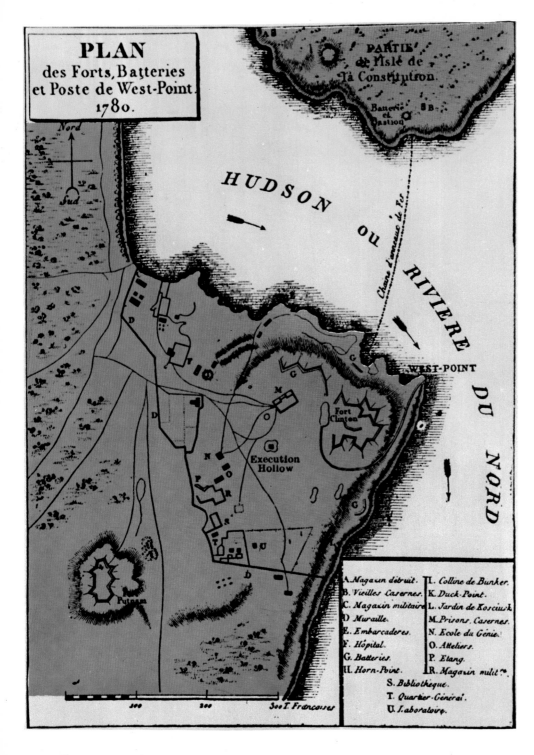

PLAN
des Forts, Batteries
et Poste de West-Point.
1780.

Nord

Sud

HUDSON OU RIVIERE DU NORD

PARTIE de l'Isle de la Constitution.

Batterie et Bastion

Chaine d'arrêteau de Fer

WEST-POINT

Fort Clinton

Execution Hollow

Putnam

A. Nagazin détruit.
B. Vieilles Casernes.
C. Magazin militaire.
D. Muraille.
E. Embarcaderes.
F. Hôpital.
G. Batteries.
H. Horn-Point.
I. Colline de Bunker.
K. Duck-Point.
L. Jardin de Kosciusk.
M. Prisons, Casernes.
N. Ecole du Génie.
O. Atteliers.
P. Etang.
R. Magazin milit.rs
S. Bibliotheque.
T. Quartier-Général.
U. Laboratoire.

100   200   300 T. Françoises

The principal engineering achievement of Thaddeus Kosciuszko in America was the design and construction in the years 1778—80 of West Point, the most formidable American fortress of that period. The fortress was to defend against an invasion from Canada by means of an on-shore system of batteries and fortifications. Here, in the course of two and a half years, under Kosciuszko's supervision a citadel (Fort Clinton), four forts situated at various levels, and various batteries and redoubts were built. The fortification plan is presented on an old map. Indicated on it is the place where a barrier in the form of a powerful chain with 60-centimeter links was stretched across the river (a fragment of that chain has been preserved down to the present — see p. 149). On the map, to the left of the legend, the letter "L" marks "Kosciuszko's Garden". There the fortifications engineer cultivated plants for his own pleasure. A view of the fortified bluffs of West Point as seen from the Hudson River is presented by an illustration from the late 18th century. Thaddeus Kosciuszko, the builder of West Point, was honored by a commemorative plaque contributed by the people of Chicago

West Point viewed from the North as it appeared at the Close of the War.

TADEUSZ KOSCIUSZKO
FEBRUARY 12, 1746
BRIGADIER GENERAL
OF
STATES ARMY 17
DER OF WEST POINT
BY CITIZENS OF
A.D. MCMXXX

A military academy, which still exists today, was founded at West Point in 1802. Through the efforts of its cadets the first monument to Thaddeus Kosciuszko in America was erected there in 1818. At present the statue of the builder of West Point graces a tall column

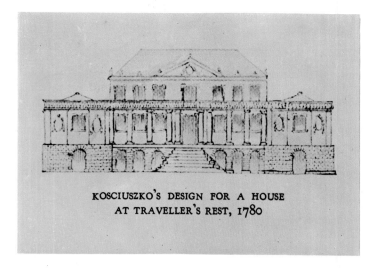

Dear Sir   *West Point 1st September*
                          1778

*I am the most enhappy man in the World, be-
cause all my Yankees the best Friends is gone
to White Plains or to Eastern and Left me
with the Mockes or Irishes impolites as the
Savages. the Satisfaction that I have at present
only is this to go all day upon the Works and
the Night to go to bed with the Cross Idea of
Lost of good Companie.
Should go to the Eastern with General Gates but
Gel. Washington was obstacle of going me there
and I am verry sorry of it.
My respect to Mistress Shayler and miss
Kayler do not forgive to your lady and
to all my Friends give my Compliments.
You must remember that if I go to Albany
I must lee in your hause.*
                          your Friend
                          Thad. Kosciuszko
                          &c

THE HON
Horatio Gates

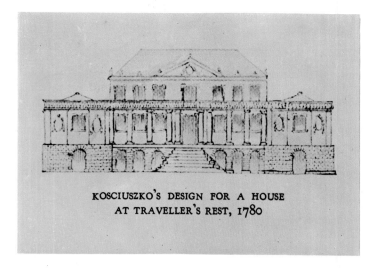

KOSCIUSZKO'S DESIGN FOR A HOUSE
AT TRAVELLER'S REST, 1780

Extended engineering work tied Kosciuszko down at West Point; meanwhile,
the main theater of the war moved to
the south. Kosciuszko sought to have
Washington place him under the command of his friend and commander at
Saratoga, Gen. Horatio Gates. That fact
is mentioned in a letter (reproduced
here) to one of his friends in which he
complained that all of his close comrades-in-arms had gone south.
None of the plans of West Point drawn
up by Kosciuszko have survived, but
several of his sketches from that period
have been preserved. They include a
portrait of Capt. Alden and an extremely interesting (though never realized) project of a private residence for
Gen. Gates at his estate of Traveller's
Rest, attesting to Kosciuszko's archi-
tectural interests

152

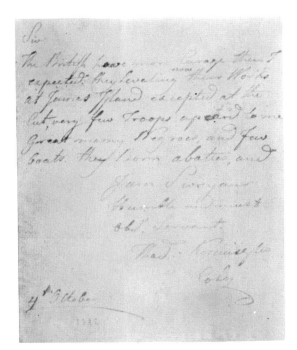

When Kosciuszko was nominated chief engineer of the Southern Army in 1780, he came under the command of Gen. Nathanael Greene who replaced Gen. Gates. Two and a half years of service in the field under guerrilla conditions in the torrid climate of South Carolina marked the final stage of Thaddeus Kosciuszko's American career. Reproduced here is one of his reports, submitted on 4 October 1782, and a portrait of Gen. Greene, under whom Col. Kosciuszko served during his final years in America

Thaddeus Kosciuszko was promoted to the rank of general of the American Army in 1783, after the war was over. As one of the commanders with the longest term of service to the cause of the American Revolution, he was decorated with the Order of the Cincinnati (see reproduction on p.133). After Kosciuszko's death, efforts were made to have the scene of his receiving that order engraved on his sarcophagus beside the scene of the oath he took as supreme commander of the 1794 Insurrection; nothing came of the project, but the sketch for such a bas-relief has survived. A personal gift of Washington to Kosciuszko was a pair of pistols, with the names of the donor and recipient together with the date 1783 and the US motto "E Pluribus unum" engraved thereon.

The portrait of Gen. George Washington presented on p. 155 was painted by John Trumbull, a contemporary artist, who immortalized on canvas a number of personnages and scenes connected with the American Revolution. He was also credited with the portrait of Kosciuszko (reproduced opposite), c. 1780, considered to be the only likeness of the Polish patriot executed during his years in America. The authenticity of this portrait is, however, occasionally questioned

154

The best-known monuments to Thaddeus Kosciuszko in the United States: one, equestrian, in Chicago (1905), the other in Washington (1910)

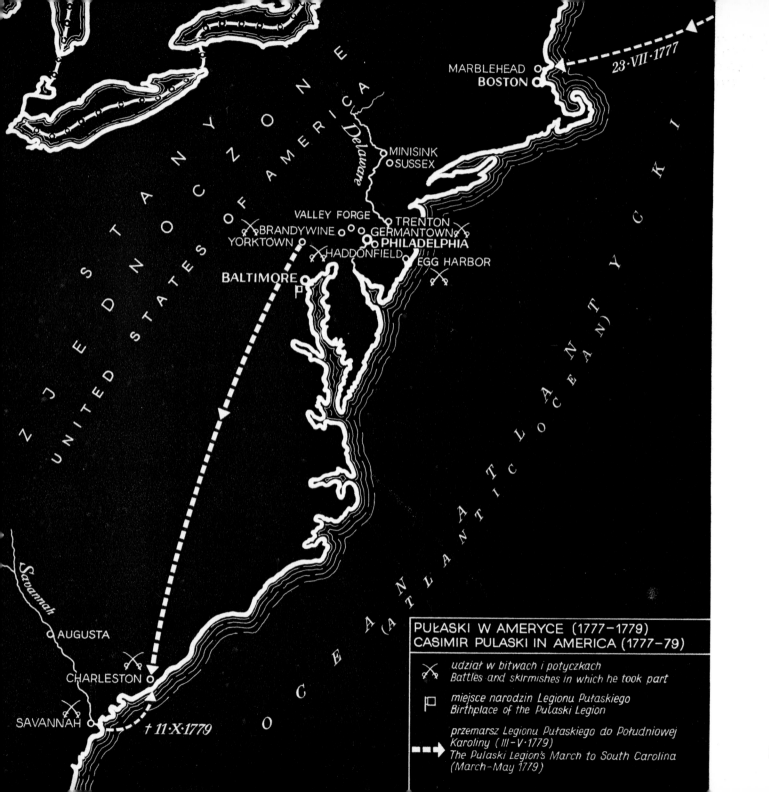

MARBLEHEAD
BOSTON
23·VII·1777

MINISINK
SUSSEX

Delaware

VALLEY FORGE
TRENTON
BRANDYWINE
GERMANTOWN
YORKTOWN
PHILADELPHIA
HADDONFIELD
EGG HARBOR
BALTIMORE
P

ZJEDNOCZONE STANY
UNITED STATES OF AMERICA

Savannah

AUGUSTA

CHARLESTON

SAVANNAH
† 11·X·1779

OCEAN ATLANTYCKI

ATLANTIC OCEAN

PUŁASKI W AMERYCE (1777–1779)
CASIMIR PULASKI IN AMERICA (1777–79)

✕ udział w bitwach i potyczkach
Battles and skirmishes in which he took part

⚑ miejsce narodzin Legionu Pułaskiego
Birthplace of the Pulaski Legion

⇢ przemarsz Legionu Pułaskiego do Południowej
Karoliny (III–V·1779)
The Pulaski Legion's March to South Carolina
(March–May 1779)

158

Casimir Pulaski according to a little-known 19th-century portrait

The Banner of the Pulaski Legion, an independent fighting force composed of cavalry and infantry, created and subsequently commanded for eighteen months by Casimir Pulaski. The Legion's "finest hours" can be seen in the valiant role it played in the Battle of Charleston and Savannah in 1779, where its commander was mortally wounded. After Pulaski's death, the Legion no longer played a major role, although it did go to form the nucleus of future US mounted formations, thereby earning its creator the title of "father of the US cavalry". Right: the saber used by Casimir Pulaski during his American sojourn and facsimile of a letter he wrote at military camp near Savannah, a month before his death

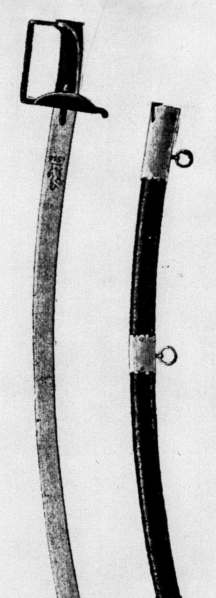

Dear General

     I have take my quarter about Seven miles from Savanah, at the widow Gibbou's house, on the way to Ogeeche's ferry, it is Very Essential post, the Ennemies got an advanced one about two miles from the town, that they have posted there Since Last night, being allarmed by the detachement wich was on their Lignes yesterday, it will be necessary that my detachement Should be reinforced not only by the Cavalry, but with Some infantry to give me the facility ot attaking their piguets, I shall pursue two miles farther on the Sunbury's road to keep a free Communication with Count D'esting, the ennemies Send on that Road Very often Some parties.

    j have the honour to be
with respect Dear General
        your most humble
        Servt
        C Pulaski

September the 14th 1779
at three o-cloK in the morning.

"General Pulaski at Savannah" (9 October 1779) painted by Stefan Batowski in 1933. Contrary to older traditions, but in accordance with source information, it is not the cavalry charge of the Legion which is depicted but only Pulaski and his adjutant among the breaking French infantry ranks near the forts defending the gates of Savannah. Leaving the Legion's rearguard, Pulaski plunged into the thick of the battle in the hope that his example might inspire the infantry to mount a similar attack, thereby clearing the way for a cavalry charge. But such an eventuality never came about. Pulaski fell mortally wounded by grapeshot. Bellow: the ball, extracted from the wound, is now on display at the Savannah Museum

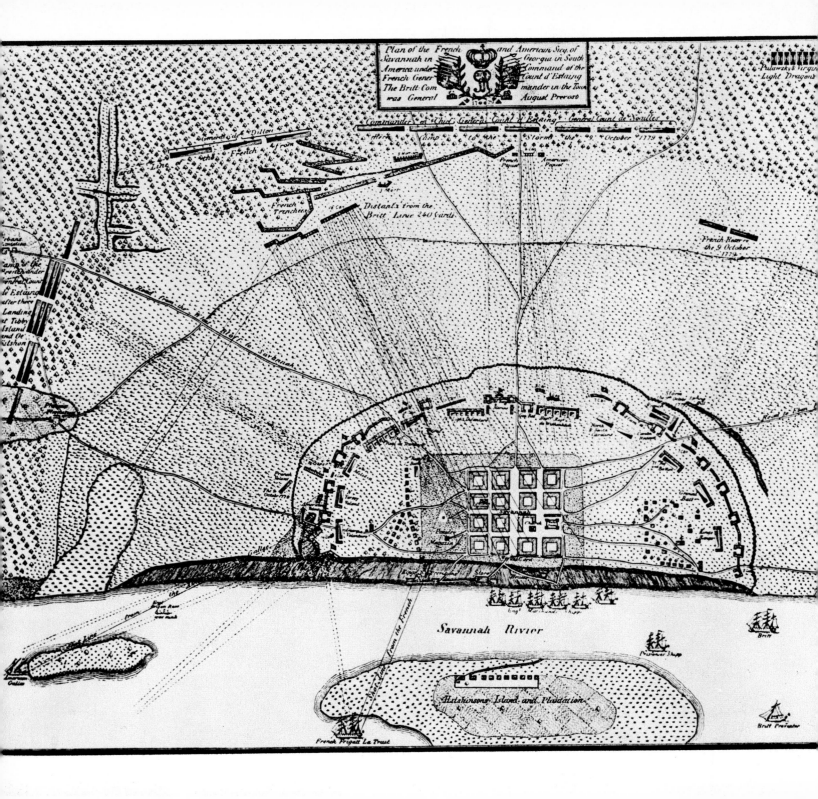

Plan of the French and American Siege of Savannah in Georgia in South America under the Command of the French General The Britt. Commander in the Town was General August Prevost

Commander at Chief General Count d'Estaing. Second Count de Noulles

Here Camp to the Storm the 9.th October 1779

Pulawsky & Virgin.s Light Dragons

French Trenches

Distant from the Britt Line 240 Yards

French Reserve the 9 October 1779

Savannah Rivier

Hutchinsons Island and Plantation

French Frigat La Trust

Britt Protector

Plan of the Battle of Savannah (illustration dating from 1779); indicated at top right is the position of the Pulaski Legion. Right: 18th-century lithograph portraying the battlefield at Savannah. In order to honor Pulaski's memory, in 1833 a fort built at the mouth of the Savannah River, near where he had been buried at sea, was named after him. Fort Pulaski, which played an important role in the American Civil War, has now been declared a National Monument

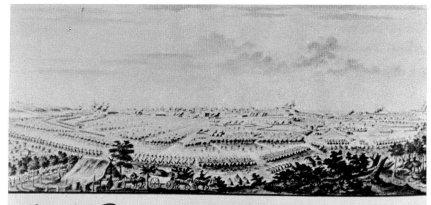

Vue de la Bille de Savannah, du Camp, des Tranchées et de L'attaque Octobre 1779.

In the mid-19th century an obelisk in honor of Casimir Pulaski wae erected at Savannah (the cornerstone had been laid in 1825). One of its bas-reliefs portrays Pulaski receiving his mortal wound. A plaqus near the monumet describes the circumstances of the hero's death.
Right: the Casimir Pulaski Monument in Washington (photo of the unveiling in 1910 and the monument as it appears today)

166

For many years now the anniversary of Casimir Pulaski's death has been solemnly observed in the United States, particularly by American Poles. As of 1969 the 11th of October has been proclaimed a holiday known as Pulaski Day in a number of states. In 1972, by official presidential proclamation, Pulaski Day became a national holiday.

Commemorative medal struck as a result of the efforts of the American Polish community on the 150th anniversary of Pulaski's death

163

Chapter V

Thaddeus Kosciuszko in the Struggle for Polish Independence

Thaddeus Kosciuszko was not in Poland on 5 August 1772 when, following the fall of the Bar Confederation, Russia, Prussia and Austria by mutual agreement effected the first partition of Poland*. The loss of nearly one third of her territory and more than one third of her population was a severe blow. Nevertheless, even after that partition, Poland still had a population of 10 millions and, with an area of half a million square kilometers, continued to be a large country by European standards. (Territorially she nearly equaled France and was three times greater than Prussia). But geographically she was situated among powerful neighbors who, after years of making encroachments on her independence, ultimately decided to partition her territory.

One of the portraits of the commander-in-chief of the insurrection, widely circulated in 1794, bore the inscription: "He severed the fetters in which the nation had groaned". Those fetters comprised not only the ever tightening chain of Poland's frontiers but also the increasing interference of foreign powers in her internal affairs. Upon his return to Poland in 1774, after five years of absence, Thaddeus Kosciuszko must have been aware of this state of affairs. His decision to leave Poland again only a year after returning from Paris was influenced mainly by personal considerations: his failure to receive a commission in the royal army and his unsuccessful marital plans. The general atmosphere prevailing in the country at that time was also conducive to this decision. As somebody no longer associated with the king's entourage, Kosciuszko must have perceived more vividly than before the extent to which Poland's independence had been restricted. That realization must have been even more poignant when in late 1784 he again reappeared in Poland after an absence of nine years, eight of which had been spent in the United States. His participation in the American Revolution, in the colonists' struggle for independence from British tyranny had provided him with considerable experience. Now he was returning from a country which had dared to assert its right to independence, to his own homeland whose sovereignty was being increasingly imperiled.

The man who was a brigadier general of the American Army, who had won acclaim in a war that had held the eyes of the world, was unable to

* See map on page 182

receive a commission in Poland's royal army, whose troop strength was limited to a mere 20,000. For five years, therefore, Kosciuszko retired to his family estate of Siechnowicze which his sister had freed of debts and saved from forfeiture. He became involved in the management of the modest estate but continued to experience financial difficulties. From time to time he would take to traveling. He was invited by the Czartoryskis to Puławy and visited the capital on several occasions. Perhaps he observed the deliberations of one of the sessions of the Great Seym in Warsaw between 1788 and 1792.

This was a period of animated political activity in Poland. Taking advantage of tsarist attention being diverted by the Russo-Turkish War, the advocates of reform attempted to force through the Seym a "basic act" aimed at changing the country's policy by strengthening the central authority of the state, liquidating the *liberum veto*, restricting the influence of the magnates and enhancing the importance of the middle strata of society (the gentry and the burgher class). The act, prepared conspiratorially by a group of patriots with the collaboration of the king, was submitted to the Seym and adopted on 3 May 1791. In effect, this amounted to a coup d'état, since the advocates of reform had hurriedly had the measure passed in defiance of procedural formalities. (Only one third of the deputies took part in those deliberations of the Seym, whose earlier than scheduled session had taken the uninformed by surprise). The act, which proclaimed Poland a constitutional monarchy of the gentry and bourgeoisie, was the world's second (after the American) constitution and the first document of its kind in Europe, preceding the adoption of the revolutionary French constitution by several months.

The Constitution of 3 May was meant to be an important step towards the reform of the Republic. It represented an attempt to strengthen the state internally and to restore the country's sovereignty. Shortly thereafter, however, native reactionary forces supported by the Empress Catherine were to attempt to overthrow the constitution.

Already in 1788 the Great Seym had strengthened the country's defense potential by a fivefold increase in the troop strength of the armed forces to 100,000. As a result of that measure, on 12 October 1789 Thaddeus Kosciuszko received the commission of major-general in the royal army. He left Siechnowicze to be stationed in a garrison at Włocławek, whence he was later reassigned to Lublin and subsequently sent to Podolia with his division, which he had drilled intensively. It was at that time that the victorious struggle to promulgate a new constitution was under way.

Within less than a year after the ratification of the Constitution of 3 May, its opponents, representatives of the Polish magnates, hatched a plot in St Petersburg, under the aegis of Catherine, to restore the old order in Poland. The conspirators came into then open on 14 May 1792 in the town of Targowica on Poland's eastern border, on the estate of Szczęsny Potocki, one of the founders of the Confederation of Targowica. The appeal by the confederates for assistance from Catherine served as a pretext for armed Russian intervention in Polish affairs. Thus began a short-lived and ill-fated struggle known as the war in defense of the May 3 Constitution which resulted in the second partition of Poland.

Four days after the proclamation of the Confederation of Targowica, a 100,000-strong Russian army invaded Poland from the south and northeast. The south-east Polish army (22,000 troops and 58 cannon), led by Lieutenant-General Prince Józef Poniatowski, a nephew of King Stanislaus Augustus, was pitted against the Russian forces (64,000 troops and 136 cannon) advancing from the Ukraine. Major-General Thaddeus Kosciuszko was the commander of one of the three divisions under Prince Poniatowski. The commander-in-chief of the entire army, in accordance with the constitution, was the king, although he remained in Warsaw far from the scene of military operations.

After two months of defensive warfare the forces of Prince Poniatowski retreated to the line of the river Bug. There the Battle of Dubienka, the first armed encounter in which Thaddeus Kosciuszko commanded, was fought to prevent the tsarist forces from crossing the river. The troops which Kosciuszko had at his disposal (5,000 soldiers against an enemy force five times as large) proved inadequate to hold back the Russians. The remaining Polish divisions had been distributed along the river at other possible crossing points. On 18 July a battle flared up at Dubienka, with Polish forces withstanding Russian attacks for five hours. This was possible owing to the fact that Kosciuszko had managed to fortify his preselected defensive positions on the western bank of the river. In that endeavor he made full use of his military-engineering skills.

He positioned three forward batteries in front of the division and ordered high earthworks thrown up to shield his infantrymen. In addition, palisades were built and the foreground was covered with "wolf pits". The battle was full of dramatic moments. Successive Russian detachments made futile attemps to penetrate the Poles' defenses, but were forced to retreat incurring considerable losses in the process.

But the battle's ultimate outcome was a foregone conclusion. In the face of overwhelming enemy odds, it was only possible to delay the advance of the tsarist forces and prevent them from surprising the remaining Polish divisions. That objective was achieved in full. The Battle of Dubienka dragged on into the late evening, and Kosciuszko's forces managed to retreat under the cover of darkness, whilst sustaining negligible losses. The tsarist army, by contrast, had suffered some 3,000 dead and wounded.

Thus the Battle of Dubienka may be termed a Polish success, and that is precisely how it was viewed by Kosciuszko's contemporaries. It marked the second successful Polish encounter with the main Russian forces, following the earlier victory of Zieleńce, where Prince Poniatowski had been in command, which, however, had engaged far fewer enemy troops. This boosted the Poles' morale and convinced them of the sense of continuing the struggle. Such was the mood of the Polish army when word arrived from Warsaw that the king had decided to join the Confederation of Targowica. Viewing further attempts to resist the tsarist forces as futile, he had hoped to save the country in this way from total disaster. In so doing he annulled the Constitution of 3 May and agreed to the government of the Targowica faction.

Among the most ardent defenders of the Constitution in the general staff of Prince Poniatowski a plan was conceived to abduct the king, remove him to a military camp and continue the struggle. There is some evidence to indicate that Thaddeus Kosciuszko was one of the originators or at least an enthusiastic supporter of that plan (an analogy may be seen here with the Bar Confederation's plot to abduct King Stanislaus Augustus, the implementation of which was to have been carried out in part by Casimir Pulaski). The plan was never put into effect owing to the opposition of Prince Józef Poniatowski who was against "doing violence to the person of the king", even though he fully shared the desire to continue the struggle. In response

172

to the king's decree calling for an end to further hostilities, Thaddeus Kosciuszko tendered his resignation together with many other officers.

Thus ended the war of 1792 in which Kosciuszko was first recognized in his native land to be a capable commander, valiant soldier and ardent patriot. For his efforts he was decorated with the Order of Virtuti Militari and promoted to the rank of lieutenant-general. An even greater distinction was the fame he won after the Battle of Dubienka which ranked him in the forefront of Poland's commanders and paved his way to the high command of the national insurrection of 1794. The name of Kosciuszko became famous throughout Poland and abroad as well, particularly in revolutionary France. On 26 August 1792 the National Legislative Assembly in Paris conferred on Kosciuszko the coveted title of "Citizen of France". Others thus distinguished for their dedication to liberty and brotherhood among nations had included George Washington.

When, as a result of the military defeat of the insurrection, the Polish government was taken over by representatives of the Targowica camp, supported by the tsarist army, many patriots left the country. Most of them turned up in Saxony, where centers of Polish émigrés, rallying opponents of Targowica, sprang up at Leipzig and Dresden. Towards the end of 1792 Kosciuszko also arrived at Leipzig.

Meanwhile in Poland a disaster, which even members of the Targowica camp had not envisaged, occurred. On the basis of an agreement between Russia and Prussia (23 January 1793), a second partition of Poland was effected, far more catastrophic than the first*. Poland's territory and population decreased two-and-a-half times. She now had slightly more than 200,000 square kilometers of area and only about 4,000,000 inhabitants as compared with 730,000 square kilometers and a population of 14,000,000 in pre-partition Poland. Only a scant semblance of independent government existed within the drastically diminished state. The Russian ambassador was the one who decided Poland's internal affairs, above the heads of the king and Seym, and his instrument of authority was the so-called Permanent Council, which was subservient to his will. 30,000 Russian troops were stationed throughout the country, with 7,000 in Warsaw alone.

___
* See map on page 182

The émigré center in Saxony, headed by Ignacy Potocki and Hugo Kołłątaj, co-authors of the Constitution of 3 May, had began to prepare for an insurrection in Poland in the beginning of 1793. Among those involved in such plans was Thaddeus Kosciuszko, who was sent to Paris to secure assistance. That mission proved unsuccessful, as the young French republic was experiencing a period of internal upheavals and facing the threat posed by the counterrevolutionary coalition. One of the fruits of Kosciuszko's sojourn at Paris was his portrait (widely circulated during the insurrection) depicting him with an upraised sword and bearing the inscription: "Let me fight for the Homeland once again." That was more than just a piece of rhetoric, since at that time thoughts of militant resistance had flared up anew in Poland and clandestine partiotic groups, vowing to throw off the tsarist yoke, were burgeoning.

At the beginning of September 1793 emissaries from Poland informed Kosciuszko at Leipzig that he had been chosen supreme commander of the planned insurgency. The conspirators, however, did not have a uniform sociopolitical program, since the membership of the underground organizations included representatives of various classes: officers, the bourgeoisie, gentry and commoners alike. The émigrés were also lacking a uniform programe. The moderate camp sought to restore Poland's territorial integrity and independence on the basis of the civil liberties guaranteed by the reactivation of the Constitution of 3 May. The more radical elements had a broader definition of what was to be meant by "freedom". Such an interpretation was exemplified by what Kosciuszko reportedly said upon being named commander-in-chief: "I shall not fight for the gentry alone. I desire the freedom of the entire nation and only for it will I risk my life."

Soon after the talks he held with the emissaries from Poland, Kosciuszko secretly made his way to the vicinity of Cracow. Both personally, and through the aid of trusted representatives, he sought to ascertain what progress had been made by the conspirators in preparing for an armed rising. He did not wish to repeat the error of the confederates and rush into an ill-prepared battle. He had frequently stressed that no insurrection could possibly hope to be successful without a 100,000-strong army. To raise such a force it was necessary, according to Kosciuszko, to enlist the support of broad segments of the nation. As a result, he decided to postpone the uprising and return to Germany, where together with Kołłątaj and Potocki in Dresden and Leipzig a socio-political program might be worked out.

In the meantime reports filtering through from Poland clearly indicated the great urgency of immediate action. The tsarist authorities had got wind of the increasingly widespread conspiracy and began arresting its leaders. At the same time a law was adopted to reduce Poland's armed forces. Any further delay threatened to deprive the insurrection of the armed potential of existing Polish garrisons scattered throughout the country. Under the circumstances, when new urgent appeals from Poland reached Dresden at the beginning of March 1794, the decision to begin operations was taken. Cracow was chosen as the place where the insurrection would be proclaimed, and General Thaddeus Kosciuszko was the first of the émigré conspirators to arrive on the scene*.

In spite of earlier plans to raise a 100,000-strong army, it became necessary to begin the insurrection with a single infantry battalion stationed at Cracow. It turned out that the day before Kosciuszko arrived in Cracow, the Russian unit stationed there had left the town. As a result, the insurrection was proclaimed without a single shot being fired. That moment occurred around noon on 24 March 1794, when in front of the local garrison and the townspeople assembled in the market place Thaddeus Kosciuszko took an oath as Supreme Commander of the Insurrection.

He swore "to the entire Polish nation" that he would never use the authority vested in him for anybody's private repression, but only for the defense of the integrity of the country's frontiers, for the restoration of the Nation's self-government and for the establishment of universal freedom. Kosciuszko hoped that the representatives of all social classes would rally round the banners of the insurrection. He considered himself the representative of the entire nation and in the interest of all citizens he would initiate a struggle for "freedom, integrity and independence". That three-part slogan was to be found on all seals of the insurrection and on all appeals and documents signed by Kosciuszko.

* See map on page 202

A week after proclaiming the insurrection Kosciuszko left Cracow and headed towards Warsaw. His force comprised 5,000 regulars and some 2,000 peasants from the Cracow countryside, hastily mobilized by special recruiters. From the very outset of the insurrection the supreme commander had appealed to the burghers and peasantry. His American experience had after all taught him that even untrained but loyal and enthusiastic units composed of peasant volunteers could be every bit as effective as regular troops. The impoverished Polish peasant, however, reduced to serfdom, had not matured to the level of a conscious citizen and considered such concepts as national solidarity wholly alien. Nonetheless, Kosciuszko succeeded in personally winning the trust of the recruits inducted into the insurrectionist camp. As a result, the peasants from the Cracow countryside felt that they had joined up with "Kosciuszko" rather than enlisting in "the Polish army". In his appeals Kosciuszko time and again would raise the question of the common folk. His most important act aimed at improving the lot of the peasantry was the proclamation, issued at his camp near Połaniec on 7 May 1794, which stated that "every peasant is free". This was a clear-cut illustration of the equal rights for all citizens guaranteed by the new Poland which was expected to emerge from the insurrection.

Even before that proclamation was issued, the peasantry had proved that they could be relied upon. They had earned their battle stripes on the twelfth day of the uprising at the Battle of Racławice (4 April 1794). On that day a column of Russian troops, despatched to Cracow to quell the insurgency, blocked the way for Kosciuszko's forces. The latter slightly exceeded the troop strength of the Russians, although the combat value of peasants armed with improvised pikes and scythes mounted upright on their shafts remained to be seen. The battle began with an indecisive clash between Polish and Russian regulars. The turning point came when Kosciuszko personally led an attack by a 320-strong unit of scythebearing volunteers. They unexpectedly emerged from a ravine in which they had lain low before an artillery barrage. The Russian batteries toward which the onslaught was directed managed to fire only two rounds before the scythebearers were upon them, capturing 12 cannon. Only 13 of the peasants lost their lives in the attack. Then Kosciuszko again led his peasants into battle to break the resistance of the tsarist force on his left flank. This attack was likewise successful and forced the Russians to flee in chaotic disarray.

Militarily the significance of the Battle of Racławice was negligible. It did not open the road for Kosciuszko's march on Warsaw, which remained blocked by the tsarist troops, which had survived the battle. In terms of political propaganda, however, this first victorious test of forces was of inestimable importance and marked a turning point in the initial phase of the insurrection. When word of the victory at Racławice reached Warsaw, an insurrection broke out there on 17 April. Within two days Poland's capital was liberated and the tsarist garrison compelled to withdraw. A week later an uprising broke out in Vilna. The hero of the Warsaw insurrection was Jan Kiliński, a cobbler from the Old Town and leader of the burghers who played an important role in the town's liberation. A Polish Jacobin, the poet Jakub Jasiński, was hailed as the hero of the uprising at Vilna.

Thus in less than a month the insurrection had turned into a nationwide movement encompassing the regions of Cracow, Warsaw and Vilna. Kosciuszko had indeed become the nation's leader. His name was now on the lips of all Poles. This is how Józef Maksymilian Ossoliński, the writer and political activist, characterized Kosciuszko after a meeting with him at the insurrectionist military camp at Cracow: "He is unpretentious and humble in speech, manners and dress. He combines a great deal of level-headed calculation and reason with resoluteness and ardent dedication to the cause. ... As regards details of execution he leaves nothing to chance; everything is calculated and planned. Perhaps his mind is not very transcendental nor sufficiently flexible for politics. But his innate common sense suffices for him to correctly assess a given situation and make the proper decision at first glance. He is animated by his love of the Homeland, and no other passion holds sway over him. ... The enthusiasm he generates in the camp and throughout the nation is incredible."

Never before had any Pole succeeded in gaining such widespread authority as Kosciuszko, to whom historians would later refer as "a dictator by the will of the people". But the course of events depended on military rather than moral successes, and the situation in that sphere had become dramatically tense. Kosciuszko had expected to fight against only the Russians, but at the next battle on 6 June at Szczekociny he encountered Russian and Prussian forces.

He had managed to assemble some 15,000 troops under his command, but the enemy forces were nearly twice as many. The tide of battle turned against the Poles. Once again Kosciuszko thrice led his scythebearing peasants into battle, attacking the Prussian infantry, checking a cavalry charge and attacking Prussian batteries. All told, the Poles suffered some 2,000 dead and wounded (Kosciuszko himself sustaining a slight wound). The battle was a painful defeat, though not a total disaster, since the Polish forces had not been dispersed and were able to retreat in orderly fashion.

After disengaging itself from the enemy Kosciuszko's corps marched via Kielce, Radom, Warka and Raszyn towards Warsaw. In anticipation of a siege, Kosciuszko ordered that fortifications be built well in advance and personally supervised their construction. No European city thus far had ever been so extensively fortified. Another innovation was the widespread and spontaneous participation of the civilian populace in the fortification and subsequent defense of Warsaw. Once again Kosciuszko had succeeded in mobilizing the entire citizenry to battle. The heroic struggle of the people of Warsaw in 1794 established a tradition in the annals of Poland's capital which would continue to shed blood while resisting invading forces up till 1939 and 1944.

The Battle of Warsaw began on 14 July and lasted until 6 September. A 40,000-strong combined Russo-Prussian force with 250 cannon besieged the town defended by a 25,000-man army with 140 pieces of artillery, supported by civilians organized into national militia detachments. The entire defense operation was commanded by Kosciuszko who personally led the national militia into combat in the most endangered and vulnerable areas. The two-month-long defense of Warsaw, which ultimately resulted in the enemy's retreat, marked the greatest military success of the insurrection. Despite the difficulties encountered by Polish divisions fighting in Lithuania and Polesie, it suddenly seemed that the insurrection had been saved. The Prussian forces had become tied down by the insurrection which broke out in Great Poland (as the Poznań region is known). That insurgency was reinforced by a 4,000-strong corps led by Jan Henryk Dąbrowski which Kosciuszko had sent to the scene. In the east Kosciuszko decided to safeguard Poland against a new Russian offensive. To achieve that end he sought to prevent the troops of General Fersen, which were retreating from Warsaw, from joining up with the fresh reinforcements sent in by Catherine to quell the rebellion. At the head of a 7,000-strong corps Kosciuszko blocked the way for the 14,000-strong force of General Fersen and expected to be reinforced by the 4,000-man division of General Poniński specially summoned for that purpose.

Since the two Polish armies had still not joined forces, the Russians realized that swift action might tip the balance in their favor and on 10 October at dawn they launched an all-out attack with all the forces at their command. At that time the arrival of General Poniński's division could have averted defeat. Things turned out differently, however. The Poles displayed exceptional valor in repulsing successive assaults. After a six-hour battle when their ammunition had run low, they sought to silence the Russian artillery with a bayonet attack. An enemy grape-shot barrage decimated the ranks of the Third Cracow Regiment — the same unit in whose presence Kosciuszko had taken the oath on the first day of the insurrection. Next the scythe bearers plunged into battle, but that attack likewise proved no match for the Russians' artillery. To complicate things, the surviving scythebearers fled in disarray back to their own lines and broke up the ranks of a quadrangular Polish infantry formation which could not make use of its firearms under the circumstances. The Russians took full advantage of the chaos by sending their cavalry into the gap that had formed in the Poles' defenses. Kosciuszko attempted to organize a last-ditch defense with his retreating detachments, but the enemy cavalry dispersed them, dashing all hope of further Polish resistance. Among the last battle-weary survivors pursued by the Russians was Kosciuszko himself, alone and unaided. His horse stumbled while attempting to leap across a marshy ditch, pinning Kosciuszko to the ground. The fallen horseman was immediately pounced upon by Cossacks who began slashing him with spears and sabers. Only later, when they realized that their victim was the commander of the insurrection himself, did they transport the unconscious Kosciuszko to the headquarters of General Fersen. The Battle of Maciejowice ended in the total defeat of the Polish forces. Half of the Poles had been killed and some 2,000 survivors, most of them wounded, were captured by the Russians.

Had the insurrection not lost its leader at Maciejowice, that one battle would not have had to spell the end of the entire uprising. A battle-ready force of considerable size remained on alert in Warsaw alone, but three weeks after Maciejowice Poland's capital was captured by the Russians and two weeks later the entire insurrection was crushed.

Those facts attest to the great and indispensable role played by Thaddeus Kosciuszko in organizing and uniting the entire nation's forces. For 200 days (from 24 March till 10 October), he had not only been the Supreme Commander of the National Armed Forces, but also the highest moral authority and true leader of the nation.

In attempting to evaluate Kosciuszko's 200-day struggle and his contribution to the nation's history, one should distinguish between two main aspects: the social and the military. To both those fields he contributed new values as the leader and chief organizer of Poland's first nationwide insurrection which drew all social classes into a common struggle for freedom and independence He was a precursor of the wars of national liberation which the Polish nation was to wage throughout the next century up till the moment Poland regained her independence after World War I.

Thaddeus Kosciuszko in the uniform of a Polish general; this copper engraving, produced after a painting by Josef Grassi, is considered to be one of the most realistic and unidealized images of Kosciuszko at the time of the Insurrection. The inscription which reads: "He severed the fetters in which the nation had groared", endows this otherwise unpretentious portrait with a certain aura of loftiness

Onzerwał kaydany, w których ięczał Narod.

Kościuszko.

Wien bey F. X. Stöckl.

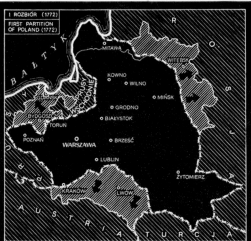

I ROZBIÓR (1772)
FIRST PARTITION OF POLAND (1772)

II ROZBIÓR (1793)
SECOND PARTITION OF POLAND (1793)

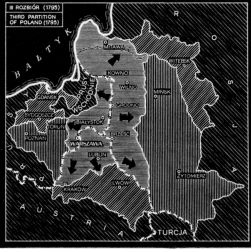

III ROZBIÓR (1795)
THIRD PARTITION OF POLAND (1795)

The French engraving reproduced here allegorically portrays the partition in 1772 of a part of Polish territory by Russia (Tsarina Catherine II), Austria (Emperor Joseph II) and Prussia (King Frederick II). The first partition (effected after the fall of the Bar Confederation) deprived Poland of 211,000 square kilometers; the second (carried out after the Russian victory over the Poles in 1792) stripped *her* of an additional 307,000 square kilometers; the third (after the fall of the Kosciuszko Insurrection) saw the remainder of Polish territory (215,000 square kilometers) divided up among the three powers. A now all but legendary protest against the first partition was the manifestation of Seym deputy Tadeusz Rejtan who barred the exit from the assembly hall to those prepared to legalize the partition. Jan Matejko captured that moment on one of his canvases. According to a highly unlikely anecdote (which Matejko did not include in his painting), Thaddeus Kosciuszko supposedly witnessed that scene, which took place on 21 April 1773, and seeing Rejtan's tragic gesture was said to have exclaimed: "There still exist virtuous and courageous souls!"

The Government Act of 3 May 1791, which later came to be known as the Constitution of 3 May was an attempt by the Patriotic Party to save the country from anarchy and foreign infiltration. The Act proclaimed Poland a constitutional monarchy, limited the influence of the conservative landed aristocracy, which had fallen under the sway of foreign interests, admitted the burgher class to participation in government and pledged greater care for the peasantry. It was Europe's first and the world's second (the first was the US Constitution of 1787) written basic law. Broad segments of Polish society enthusiastically greeted the act which promised to reform the country. Unfortunately, a year later armed intervention by Tsarist Russia put an end to the reforms. The war of 1792, often referred to as the war in defense of the constitution, ended with the second partition of Poland and the further limitation of her sovereignty. A contemporary artist, Jean-Pierre Norblin, portrayed the Seym, sitting in Warsaw's Royal Castle, promulgating the constitution on 3 May 1791

Facsimile of the first paragraphs of the memorable Constitution of 3 May. Above: signatures on the so-called bill of assurance, a document supporting the act under deliberation

On the 100th anniversary of the promulgation of the Constitution of 3 May, Jan Matejko executed a painting showing the enthusiasm with which the inhabitants of Warsaw welcomed the triumph of Poland's socio-political reformers. The painting shows the deputies having left the Royal Castle (visible in background) after the debate, proceeding to St John's Cathedral where the king was to swear in the new act. In the center of the picture we see marshal of the Seym, Stanisław Małachowski being carried shoulder high by the cheering crowd

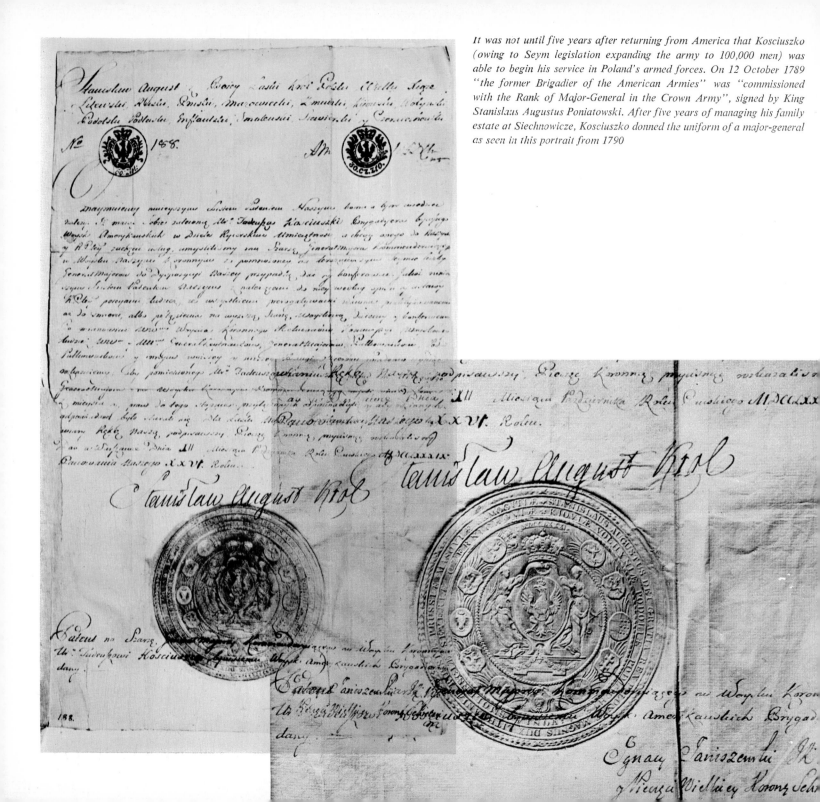

It was not until five years after returning from America that Kosciuszko (owing to Seym legislation expanding the army to 100,000 men) was able to begin his service in Poland's armed forces. On 12 October 1789 "the former Brigadier of the American Armies" was "commissioned with the Rank of Major-General in the Crown Army", signed by King Stanislaus Augustus Poniatowski. After five years of managing his family estate at Siechnowicze, Kosciuszko donned the uniform of a major-general as seen in this portrait from 1790

During the Polish-Russian War of 1792 Kosciuszko personally commanded one of the Polish divisions. He gained renown at the Battle of Dubienka on 18 July 1792, the greatest battle of the entire campaign. Owing to good fortifications and the proper deployment of artillery, the Polish troops, although outnumbered five to one, succeeded in effectively containing the main enemy forces and retreating under the cover of darkness. Both portraits presented here pay tribute to the hero of Dubienka. Left: a portrait by an unknown artist depicting Kosciuszko against the backdrop of field fortifications (not visible in the reproduction) and flashing artillery. Perhaps this portrait served as a pattern for the French artists who portrayed "the general of the Polish revolutionary army of 1792" in knight's armor (compare the illustration presented here with the "Jacobin portrait" on p. 27)

KOSCIUSZKO.
Général de l'Armée Révolutionnaire
Polonaise en 1792.

Major-General Thaddeus Kosciuszko was among the first to be decorated by the king with the newly created Order of Virtuti Militari. Originally the order was in the form of a medal, later it took on the appearance of a cross. This etching of 1792, like many other portraits of Kosciuszko, shows the Cross of Virtuti Militari presented to him in July 1792. Kosciuszko was also promoted to the rank of lieutenant-general. On 30 July 1792, in protest against the king's order to cease hostilities and his joining of the Targowica camp (enemies of the constitution bent on appeasing Tsarist Russia), Thaddeus Kosciuszko, together with other officers of the royal army, tendered his resignation. Reproduced here is the "Note to His Majesty" in this matter

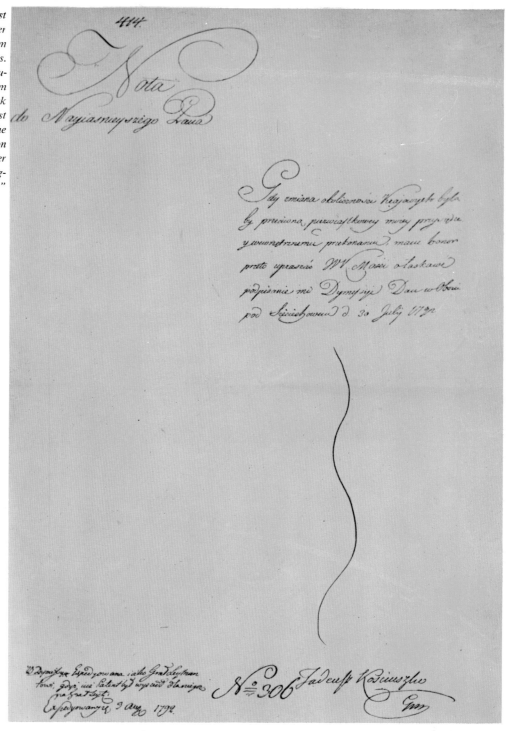

Stolnikowo Dobrodziń

792   184.

Pozytam Konie i Rzeczy chcieysz alokowac
usiebie. Konie zas możesz wszystkie przedac
Procz Kasztanowatego Konia, i czarnego.
Siwadcy Klaczy, i Siwego, ktore chce
Konserwowac, ia mogę Zimo przeżyie
chie albo predzey idzie to do okoliczz
ności, prosze wszythim sie klaniac i
będz przekonana o moiey Stałey przy
iazni, affekcie, i Sercu w nostaly nym
bynay Zdrowa. Woiciuszku
chociby ita mo to przeday
konie ——

In the fall of 1792 Kosciuszko prepared to leave Poland for Saxony and there join up with Polish émigrés intending to continue the fight for Polish independence. Reproduced is a letter written by Kosciuszko just prior to this departure; addressed to his sister, Anna Estkowa, it contains instructions concerning the management of his small family estate at Siechnowicze and announcing his intention of returning. Eighteen months later he was to return as leader of the insurrection, though he was never again to see the places of his childhood.

The drawing by Aleksander Orłowski depicting Kosciuszko on horseback

Tadeusz Kościuszko.
Dobry y waleczny
lecz nieszczęśliwy

Maria Anna of Württemberg née Czartoryska and her
mother Izabela Czartoryska

Kosciuszko **left** Warsaw and in October 1793 traveled south to the Austrian partition, where the Polish community greeted him enthusiastically as the hero of the recent struggle. He spent his name-day (28 October) at Sieniawa, the estate of Prince Czartoryski near Rzeszów, who already at that time considered Kosciuszko to be the man predestined to play the key role in the fight against the invading powers. Political calculation on the part of the Czartoryski family gave rise to a proposal to link Kosciuszko in wedlock to the Czartoryskis' daughter, Maria of Württemberg. A memento of that period is the likeness of Kosciuszko, sketched by Maria and signed sentimentally by her mother, Princess Izabela.

In December 1793, using the pseudonym Tadeusz Bieda, Kosciuszko arrived in Wrocław. He failed to receive permission for an extended stay from the Austrian authorities and left for Leipzig

On 24 March 1794, as the commander-in-chief of the National Army Kosciuszko proclaimed an insurrection. In the market place of Cracow, whither he had come a day earlier at the bidding of Polish conspiratorial circles, he took an oath of allegiance.

The oath-taking scene was portrayed by the Cracow painter, Michał Stachowicz, who may have personally witnessed the event. He painted over a dozen pictures on the same subject, which differ only in details

PRZYSIĘGA

Wykonana przez TADEUSZA KOSCIUSZKĘ Naywyższego Naczelnika Siły zbroyney Narodowey.

Ja TADEUSZ KOSCIUSZKO przysięgam w obliczu Boga całemu Narodowi Polskiemu, iż powierzoney mi władzy, na niczyi prywatny ucisk nieużyię, lecz iedynie iey dla obrony całości granic, odzyskania samowładności narodu, i ugruntowania powszechney wolności używać będę. Tak mi Panie Boże dopomoż i niewinna męka Syna iego.

Equestrian portrait of the commander-in-chief of the National Army by Michał Stachowicz. Owing to their attention to historical detail, his paintings are of great documentary value. Artistically speaking they tend to be somewhat primitive, which also in a way endows them with a certain charm. (See reproductions on preceding page and on pp. 210, 211 and 228).

A high level of graphic artistry was represented by the engravings done by foreign artists during the initial months of the insurrection: the English engraving, cast on 3 June 1794, was based on the portrait of Kosciuszko painted during his stay at Leipzig; the Dutch copper engraving was executed on the basis of Josef Grassi's portrait of 1794. The latter is credited with several portraits of the commander-in-chief; a striking feature of this portrait is the "liberty cap" associated with the French Revolution; moreover, the Dutch engraver enriched the portrait's symbolism by embellishing its border with a saber, shackles and a laurel branch

Thaddeo Kosciusko,

GENERAL IN CHIEF

of the Revolutionary Army in Poland.

After an original drawing by Schroeder, made
at Leipzig during his residence in that City.

THADDEUS KOSCIUSZKO,

GENERAL EN CHEF,

des Armées Polonaises

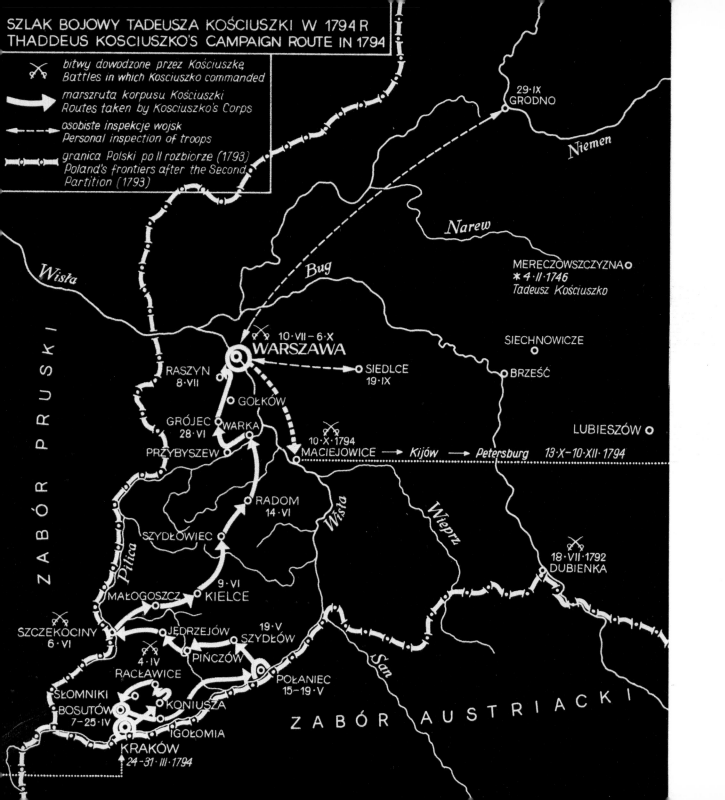

SZLAK BOJOWY TADEUSZA KOŚCIUSZKI W 1794 R
THADDEUS KOSCIUSZKO'S CAMPAIGN ROUTE IN 1794

bitwy dowodzone przez Kościuszkę
Battles in which Kosciuszko commanded

marszruta korpusu Kościuszki
Routes taken by Kosciuszko's Corps

osobiste inspekcje wojsk
Personal inspection of troops

granica Polski po II rozbiorze (1793)
Poland's frontiers after the Second
Partition (1793)

Wisła

Niemen

29·IX
GRODNO

Narew

Bug

MERECZOWSZCZYZNA o
* 4·II·1746
Tadeusz Kościuszko

SIECHNOWICZE

⚔ 10·VII – 6·X
WARSZAWA

RASZYN
8·VII

BRZEŚĆ

o SIEDLCE
19·IX

GOŁKÓW

GRÓJEC
28·VI

WARKA

LUBIESZÓW o

PRZYBYSZEW

⚔ 10·X·1794
MACIEJOWICE → Kijów → Petersburg   13·X–10·XII·1794

Z
A
B
Ó
R

P
R
U
S
K
I

RADOM
14·VI

Wisła

SZYDŁOWIEC

Pilica

Wieprz

⚔ 18·VII·1792
DUBIENKA

9·VI
MAŁOGOSZCZ   KIELCE

⚔ SZCZEKOCINY
6·VI

JĘDRZEJÓW

19·V
SZYDŁÓW

⚔ 4·IV
RACŁAWICE

PIŃCZÓW

San

SŁOMNIKI

BOSUTÓW
7–25·IV

KONIUSZA

POŁANIEC
15–19·V

Z A B Ó R   A U S T R I A C K I

IGOŁOMIA

KRAKÓW
24–31·III·1794

202

Pozwol ieszcze raz bić się za Oyczyznę.

TADEUSZ KOSCIUSZKO

NAYWYŻSZY

NACZELNIK

SIŁY ZBROYNEY NARODOWEY.

Gdy Polska pod Przemocą swe jestestwo traci;
Gdy odrodek zdradliwy przedaie swych Braci,

Na odgłos jęk serc czułych, Kościuszko przybywa;
Do broni, do wolności, cały Narod wzywa.

Bić Woyska Nieprzyiacioł, ten Naczelnik Prawy.
Oczyścić ziemię z Zdraycow, szukać każe sławy.

w Drukarni X. Mejera.

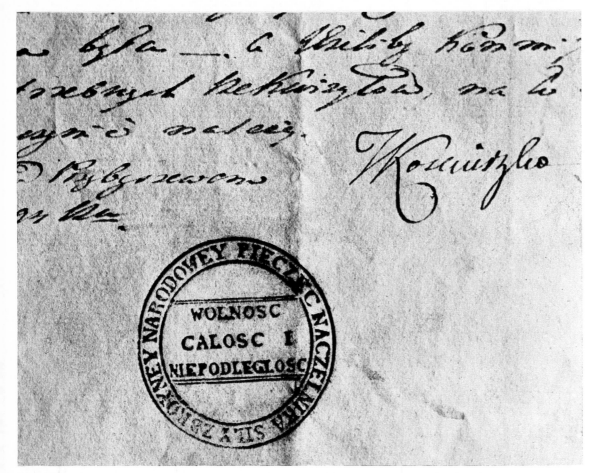

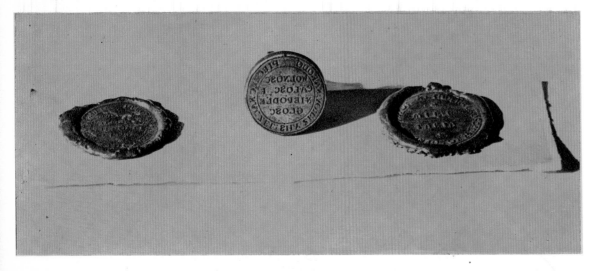

AKT

POWSTANIA OBYWATELOW, MIESZKANCOW WOIEWODZTWA KRAKOWSKIEGO.

Wiadomy iest światu stan teraźnieyszy nieszczęśliwey Polski. Niegodziwość dwoch sąsiedzkich Mocarstw i zbrodnia Zdraycow Oyczyzny, pogrążyły ią w te przepaść. Uwzięta na zniszczenie Imienia Polskiego, Katarzyna II, w zmowie z wiarołomnym Fryderykiem Gwilelmem, dokonała zamiarow nieprawości swoiey. Nie masz rodzaiu fałszu, obłudy i podstępu, ktoremi by się te dwa rządy nie splamiły, dla dogodzenia swoiey zemście i chciwości. Ogłaszaiąc się bezwstydnie Carowa za gwarantkę całości, niepodległości i szczęścia Polski, rozrywała i dzieliła Jey Kraie, znieważała Jey niepodległość, trapiła bezustannie wszelkiego rodzaiu klęskami. Gdy zaś Polska zbrzydziwszy sobie jey obelżywe iarzmo, odzyskała Prawa samowładności swoiey, użyła przeciwko niey zirayowOyczyzny, bezbożny ich spisek wsparła całą swą mocą zbroyną, a chytrze od obrony Kraiu odwiodłszy Krola, ktoremu Seym prawy i Narod wszyskie siły swoie powierzył, wkrotce samychże zdraycow haniebnie zdradziła. Przez takie podstępy stawszy się Panią losow Polski, wezwała do łupow Fryderyka Gwilelma, nadgradzaiąc iego wiarołomstwo, w odstąpieniu nayuroczystszego z Rzecząpospolitą traktatu. Pod wymyślonemi pozorami, ktorych fałsz i bezczelność samym tylko tyranom przystoi, w istocie zaś dogadzaiąc nienasyconey chciwości i chuci, rozpostarcia tyranii przez opanowanie przyległych Narodow; zagarnęły te dwa spiknione na Polskę Mocarstwa, odwieczne i niezaprzeczone Dziedzictwa Rzeczypospolitey, otrzymały na zbrodniczym zieździe zatwierdzenie zaborow swoich, wymusiły przysięgi na poddaństwo i niewolą, wkładaiąc naysroższe na Obywatelow obowiązki, a sami żadnych procz arbitraluey woli nie znaiąc; oznaczyły zuchwale, nowym i niesłychanym dotąd w Prawie Narodow ięzykiem, illność Rzeczypospolitey w rzędzie państw niższego stopnia; okazuiąc iawnie, że tak prawa iak granice państw udzielnych od ich upodobania zawisły, i że patrzą na pułnocną Europę, iak na łup przeznaczony dla ich drapieżnego despotyzmu.

Pozostała resata Polski, nie okupiła tak strasznemi klęskami polepszenia stanu swego. Ukrywaiąc Carowa niebespieczne Europeyskim Mocarstwom dalsze zamiary swoie, poświęciła ią tym czasem barbarzyńskiey i nieukoioney zemście. Depce w niey nayświętsze Prawa Wolności, bespieczeństwa, własności Osob i maiątkow Obywatelskich; myśli i czucia poczciwego Polaka, nie znaydują schronienia przed iey podeyrzliwym prześladowaniem: mowie samey więzy narzuciła. Zdraycy tylko Oyczyzny maią od niey pobłażanie, aby się bezkarnie wszelkich dopuszczali zbrodni. Rozszarpali oni maiątek i dochody publiczne, wydarli obywatelską własność, podzielili między siebie Urzędy kraiowe, iak gdyby łupy na pokonaney Oyczyznie zdobyte; a przybrawszy sobie świętokradzko imie Narodowego rządu, wszystko gwoli obcey tyranii i na pierwsze iey skinienie, niewolniczo dopełniaią. Rada Nieustaiąca, twor obcego narzutu, prawą Narodu wolą zniesiona, a świeżo od zdraycow na nowo wskrzeszona, targa, na rozkaz Posła Moskiewskiego, te nawet granice władzy swoiey, ktore od tegoż Posła z podłością przyieła, gdy ledwie co zniesione, lub uchwalone ustawy samowolnie podnosi, przerabia i niszczy. Słowem, Rząd mniemany Narodu, Wolność, bespieczeństwo i własność Obywatelow, zostaią w ręku niewolniko w-słuzi Carowy, ktorey przemagaiące w kraiu Woyska, są tarczą dla ich nieprawości.)1(

The Act of Insurrection, a basic political document outlining Poland's situation and proclaiming an uprising, was drawn up abroad at Leipzig and Dresden by two of the most active conspirators, Hugo Kołłątaj and Ignacy Potocki. The ratification and signing of this document took place in the Town Hall in the Cracow market place. Shown is the hall in which that event occurred. (This hall no longer exists, as the only remaining vestige of the Town Hall is its tower)

206

Tadeusz
Kościuszko.

Najwyższy Naczelnik Siły zbrojnej Narodowej do Obywatelów.

Wiyci Obywatele Wzywam po tylokrotnie Do Was do Ratowania
kochanej Oyczyzny. Stawam na Czele podług Waszey Woli.

[...]

Thaddeus Kosciuszko's proclamation "To The Citizenry", issued on the eve of the insurrection (a contemporary manuscript), and the texts of proclamations "To the Army" and "To Polish Women", published in the Warsaw insurrectionary gazette in April 1794, after the liberation of the capital. The proclamation to the citizenry reads in part as follows: "This is the last moment in which despair, amid shame and disgrace, places weapons in our hands. In a contempt for death lies the sole hope of improving our lot and that of future generations. Let us not succumb to the terror brought to bear by enemies who plot our ruin. The first step towards throwing off our yoke is to dare to be free. The first step towards victory is to be aware of one's own strength".

A miniature portrait of the commander-in-chief in an ornate frame used to adorn the soldiers' bandoleers

---

4 t

DODATEK DO NRU 5.
GAZETY
POWSTANIA POLSKI.

Z Warszawy Dnia 29. Kwietnia.

DALSZE PROKLAMACYE y ROZRZĄDZENIA KRAKOWSKIE.

(*Reszta Odezwy Kościuszki do Woyska.*)

winniście. Ona na Was woła o obronę; ia w Jey Imieniu moie Wam przesyłam rozkazy.

Biorę z Wami ukochani Koledzy za Hasło Smierć! albo Zwycięstwo! ufam Wam i temu Narodowi, który zginąć raczey postanowił, a niżeli dłużey ięczeć w haniebney niewoli.

TADEUSZ KOSCIUSZKO.
mpp.

— *Odezwa tegoż. do Kobiet Polskich.*

TADEUSZ KOSCIUSZKO NACZELNIK NAYWYZSZY SIŁY ZBROYNEY NARODOWEY.

Ozdobo Rodzaiu ludzkiego Płci piękna! cierpieó szczerze na widok niespokoyney twey troskliwości, o los śmiałego przedsięwzięcia, które ku oswobodzeniu Oyczyzny przedsiębiorą Polacy i łzy wasze, które wam tu troskliwość z serc czułych wyciska, przeymuie serca Rodaka waszego ogólnemu szczęściu poświęcaiącego się z Rozkoszą.

Pozwolcie mi podać wam Wspoł-Obywatelki; moią myśl, w którey się znayduie i dogodzenie czułości Waszey i dogodzenie potrzebie Publiczney. Tak iest los ludzkości nieszczęśliwy, iż ani Praw swoich utrzymać, ani Praw Narodu odzyskać nie można, bez przykrych i kosztownych sercom tkliwym offiar! Bracia, Synowie wasi, bić się idą, krew nasza musi wasze upewnić szczęścia kobiety; niech oney wylew wasze wstrzymaią starania? Raczcie proszę was na miłość ludzkości robić harpie i bandaże dla Woyska, Offiara ta Rąk pięknych, ulży cierpieniom i męstwo same zachęci.

TADEUSZ KOSCIUSZKO.

G —Uchwa-

Kosciuszko's armies in the process of forming detachments in localities of the Cracow area (April 1794). Kosciuszko is shown in both paintings: at the camp near Bosutów he is depicted among scythe-bearing peasant insurrectionists; at the camp at Igołomia he is portrayed on horseback reviewing his troops as they march past. Both paintings were the work of Michał Stachowicz done ten years after the insurrection

The banner of 1794 bears a characteristic slogan: "When he wants to defend himself, not to oppress others, the Pole's motto is death or victory".
Right: A 19th-century reconstruction of the uniforms worn by various formations of Kosciuszko's army

213

ŻYWIĄ Y BRONIĄ

Original banner of the Cracow grenadiers (scythebearers), given to the battalion by Kosciuszko on 16 July 1794 in Warsaw, bears a device that was also to be famous in later years. It recalls that the peasants are those who "feed and defend" the country.

Right: Reproduction from a brochure containing instructions on the use of a new weapon (the lance and scythe) which turned out to be quite deadly in the hands of peasants; the brochure was issued in 1794

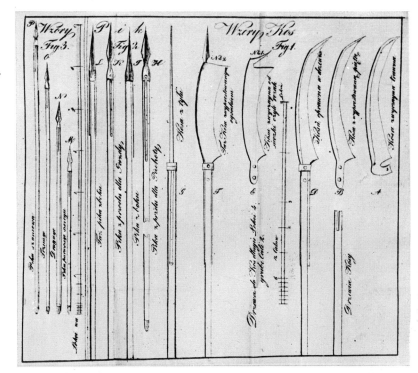

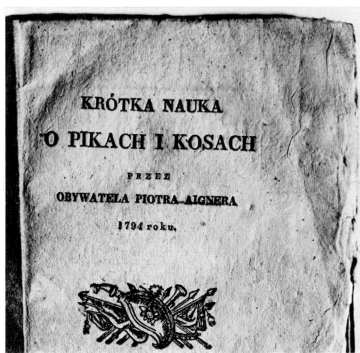

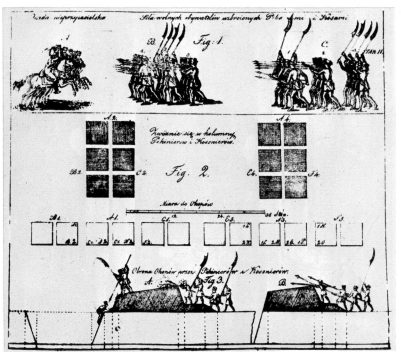

The Battle of Racławice was fought on 4 April 1794, on the twelfth day of the insurrection. It brought fame mainly to the scythebearers, peasants from the villages around Cracow, whose daring attack on Russian batteries proved decisive to the Poles' victory. The drawings reproduced here depict the attack of the scythebearers; one of them shows Kosciuszko in the background (wearing a hat) personally leading peasants into battle. Both drawings were the work of Aleksander Orłowski.

The battle plan is after an 18th-century sketch

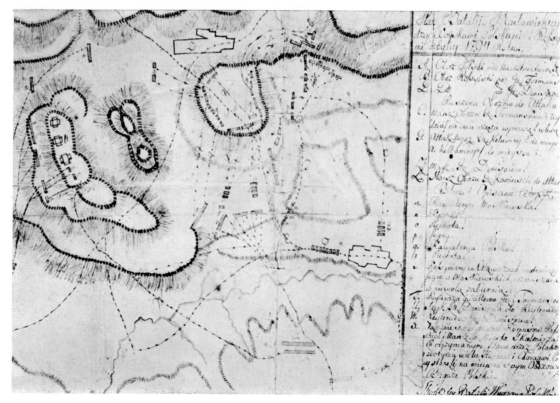

The Battle of Racławice, particularly the part played in it by the peasantry, became the subject of many paintings. Juliusz Kossak (1824—99) portrayed Kosciuszko against a background of attacking scythebearers; his son, Wojciech Kossak (1857—1942), depicted a column of scythebearers leaving a ravine and going into battle.
Below: A painting by Józef Chelmoński (1849—1914) showing the scythebearers at prayer on the battlefield at Racławice

219

A monumental work in tribute to the victory at Racła-wice was the "Racławice Panorama", painted by Woj-ciech Kossak and Jan Styka to commemorate the 100th anniversary of the battle. The huge canvas with an area of 1,800 square meters (120 meters long, 15 meters high) was put on display in 1894 at Lvov in a rotunda specially built for the purpose. The artistic setting was so arranged as to make it impossible for beholders to recognize where the three-dimensional set ended and the painting began. (This may be seen from the accompanying photograph showing the crea-tors against the background of a part of their work). The painting, of which fragments are presented here, was damaged during World Wars I and II. Since 1945, after being moved from Lvov to Wrocław, the painting has been renovated. The photograph on the opposite page provides some indication of its monumental size. When the conservation work is over the Racławice Panorama will be displayed at a pavilion which is to be constructed specially for this purpose in Cracow near the Kosciuszko Mound

Poland's most outstanding historical painter, Jan Matejko (1838—93), devoted one of the works of his epic series on the history of Poland to Racławice. "Kosciuszko at Racławice" has been on display at the National Museum in Cracow ever since 1888 and ranks among the most valuable of historical mementoes. As was the case with all of Matejko's paintings, the critics disapproved of a certain theatricality in the portrayal. Also criticized were the poor likeness of Kosciuszko and his American-style corded uniform as opposed to the peasant coat in which he had been traditionally portrayed. The painting depicts a post-battle scene with two of principal heroes. Left: Kosciuszko on horseback, right: Bartosz Głowacki standing beside a cannon captured from the Russians. A critic of the day wrote of "Kosciuszko at Racławice": "There were two heroes of the victory immortalized by our master: on the left, riding past a forest, is the commander-in-chief who has stopped for a moment and removed his cap to listen to the enthusiastic shouts of the peasantry; to the right is Głowacki. standing bareheaded beside a cannon beneath a church banner erect, serious and tranquil as behooved one who, deeming himself a citizen of the land, through his military effort came to rank among the most noble in the nation. There are two heroes, but that does not undermine the unity of action, for the spirit and thoughts of both are one"

Kosciuszko's group (detail from Matejko's painting)

Bartosz Glowacki's group (detail from Matejko's painting)

Kołłątaj's group (detail from Matejko's painting)

A group of cheering scythebearers (detail from Matejko's painting)

Three days after the Battle of Racławice pieces of artillery captured from the Russians were triumphantly displayed in the Cracow market place. Their entry was portrayed by Michał Stachowicz. On the battlefield of Racławice directly after the victory Kosciuszko reportedly donned a peasant coat to express his gratitude to the heroic scythe-bearers, and made the most courageous of them, Wojciech Bartosz-Głowacki, an officer: the event is depicted by a wood engraving from the mid-19th century.

In recognition of the role of the peasantry in society, on 7 May 1794, a month after the Battle of Racławice, a proclamation was issued at the camp near Połaniec. It stated that "every peasant is a free man". The Proclamation of Połaniec, whose full text is shown on a contemporary poster, marked the first step towards granting equal rights to the peasants. Although never actually implemented owing to the collapse of the insurrection, it remained a symbol of the progressive program of the insurrectionists

TADEUSZ KOSCIUSZKO
NAYWYZSZY NACZELNIK SIŁY ZBROYNEY NARODOWEY.

DO KOMMISSYI PORZĄDKOWYCH WSZYSTKICH ZIEM I POWIATOW

Nigdyby Polakom broń Ich Nieprzyiaciół straszną nie była, gdyby sami pomiędzy sobą zgodni znali swą siłę, i całey tey siły użyć umieli, nigdy by mówię orężem Polaków pokonać nie można, gdyby chytry nieprzyiaciel przewrotnością, zdradą, i podstępami, to naszczęi i chęci sposobu oporu. Cały ciąg Tyranii Moskiewskiey w Polszcze iest dowodem do iakiego stopnia ta przemoc miała losem Naszym, i używaiąc kiedy przekupstwa, zwodniczych przyrzeczeń, pochlebstwa przesadne, pochlebstwa namiętności, kurseaia iednych przeciwko drugim, czernienia u obcych, wszystkiego słowem co złość piekielna z chytrością a nieprzewrotnicią się połączono wymycić mie.

W tylokrotnych zdarzeniach w których Polacy do broni, przeciw niey się porywali, możeż ten Ród zboynikow liczyć iedno nad niemi praw dziwe zwycięstwo ? a przecież zawsze koniec śmiała i Polskiey był ten, że zwyciężony nieprzyiaciel wracał na karki Zwycięzcom iarzmo na moment ułożone. Zkąd więc pochodzi ta klątwa Kraiów Polskich obrot? czemu ten Naród ieczał bez sposobu wydobycia się? oto ztąd że chytre Moskiewskich Intrygi mocnieysza niż broń, gubiła zawsze Polaków z ich Polakami.

Dzielił nas nieszczęśliwych Polków mniemania Rządowe i Opinie względem tem prawideł, na których bez wolności organizacyi Narodu gruntować winny być, a do niewinney Opinii różnicy występny duch miłości własney i osobistych widoków, musiał upor, zwłokę i błędność uwzięciania się z Obcemi, a zatym podległe Onym uległania.

Czas przyszedł dopełnienia miary nieszczęść i cierpień przyspieszony, czas oświecenia iskrę Polski Epoka, w którym ieden cel, ieden niewątpliwy i sprzeczne podpaść nie mogący zamiar, zjednoczyć powinien serca i umysły, i nie zostawić od związku ogólnego oddzielnych Polaków, chyba Zdrayców uznanych, lub lękliwych i niepewnych i woli Narodu stanowić pod iakim on sechce bydź Rządem Powod więc rozmaitości Opinów zawieszony, a cel Swięty i oczewisty czyni dziś nie nad sercami, i zbiera do kupy tych nawet, co ich wieloraki dotąd różnić mogły przyczyny.

Czas ten przeto albo raczey Jego moment, chwyconey bydź ina z nieprzyiaciel całą moc swoią, siły przeszkodzić korzystaniu z tey pory, użyie broni, lecz ie mieć można za naymniey niebezpieczne przemocy Jego narzędzie, naprzeciw kupie strwożonych iuż niewolników, posławszy małe potężną swobodnych Mieszkańców, którzy o własne szczęście walczące, nie mogą chybić zwycięstwa: a w czem nas dotąd pokonywał, to narzędzie gdzini miałkiem gryzących, ten ćmierzły Machiawelismu przemysł, pokona barzność Nasza, gorliwość Poczciwych Obywatelów i groźny miecz Sprawiedliwości, który dosięgnie wszędzie, gdzie się zdrada lub przewrotność szkodliwa Narodowi okaże.

Lostedy Polski od tego zawisł, abyśmy skruszyli podwoyną siłę nieprzyiaciół Naszych, to iest: siłę orężna i siłę intryg. Winienem przeto podać wiadomości Narodowey te Moskale szukaią sposobow poburzenia Wieyskiego Ludu, przeciwko Nam, wystawuiąc Mu Artur Inosć Panów, dawnych nędze, i na koniec pomnieyszą przyszłość za pomocą Moskiewską. To mówiąc zachęcaią i przypuszczaią Lud Wieyski do wspólnego Dworów rabunku. Prostota częstokroć potrzebą omylona, może wpadać i wpada w samey rzeczy w te sidła, a nawet iuż iest doświadczenie, że uwiedzionych czy gwałtem wziętych w mundury swoie ubieraia.

Z żalem to wyznać muszę iż często srogie obchodzenie się z Ludem, daie niegodnym Moskalom do powszechney na cały Naród potwarzy. Odbi-ram ustawiczne skargi od Żołnierzy i Rekrutów że Żonych ich Dzieci nie tylko żadnego osłodzenia nie maią, ale zato prawe że służą Rzeczypospolitey ich Mężowie i Oycowie wystawieni są na naywiększe uciążliwości. Takowe postępki w wielu Mieyscach są zapewne bez wiedzy i przeciw woli Dziedziców, lecz w drugich muszą bydź skutkiem złey chęci, lub obcego natchnienia, aby zupełnie zapał od obrony Oyczyzny w sercach Ludu ostudzić.

Ale Ludzkość Sprawiedliwość i dobro Oyczyzny, wskaznie Nam łatwe i pewne środki, przez które podstępom złości domowey, lub zagraniczney Intrygi zapobiedz możemy. Rzeknimy że Lud niedopiero zostaie pod opieką Rządu Kraiowego, że uczyniony Człowiek ma gotową ucieczkę do Kommisyi Porządkowey swego Woiewodztwa, że Ciemięzyciel Prześladowca Obrońców, Kraiu iako nieprzyiaciel z i333nym Oyczyzny karany będzie. Sposob ten z Sprawiedliwością wspaniałego Narodu zgodny, duszom tkliwym miły, a osobistemu Interessowi lekka tylko kosztuiący Offiarę, przywiąże Lud do sprawy publiczney, i uchroni go od sideł nieprzyiacielskich. Zalecam przeto Kommissyom Porządkowym Woiewodztw i Ziem w całym Kraiu aby następuiące Urządzenie do wszystkich Dziedziców Posessorów i miejsce Ich zastępuiących Rządcow wydały.

1mo. Ogłosi Ludowi iż podług Prawa zostaie pod Opieką Rządu Kraiowego.

2do. Że Osoba wszelkiego Włościanina iest wolna, i że mu wolno przenieść się gdzie chce, byleby oświadczył Kommisyi Porządkowey swego Woiewodztwa gdzie się przenosi, i byleby długi winne oraz Podatki Kraiowe opłacił.

3tio. Że Lud ma ulżenie w robociznach tak iż en który robi dni 5 lub 6 w Tygodniu ma mieć dwa dni opuszczone w Tygodniu, Który robił dni 3 lub 4 w Tygodniu ma mieć opuszczony dzień ieden, kto robi dni 2 ma mieć opuszczony dzień ieden. Kto robił w Tygodniu dzień ieden, ma teraz robić w dwóch Tygodniach dzień ieden. Do tego kto robił Pańszczyznę po dwoie, maią mu bydź opuszczone dni po dwoie. Kto robił po iednemu, maią mu bydź dni opuszczone poiedynczo. Takowe opuszczanie trwać będzie przez czas Insurrekcyi poki w czasie władza Prawodawcza stałego w tey mierze urządzenia nie uzżyi.

4to. Zwierchności Mieyscowe starać się będą aby tych którzy zostaią w Woysku Rzeczypospolitey Gospodarstwo nie upadło, i żeby Ziemia która iest żrodłem bogactw Naszych odłogiem nie leżała, do czego równie Dwory iako i Gromady przykładać się powinny.

5to. Od tych którzy będą wezwani na Pospolite Ruszenie, poki tylko będą zostawać pod bronią, Pańszczyzna przez ten czas nie będzie wyciągana, lecz dopiero rozpocznie się d powrotem Ich do Domu.

6to. Własność posiadanego gruntu z obowiązkami do niego przywiązanemi podług wyżey wyrażoney ulgi, nie może bydź od Dziedzica żadnemu Włościaninowi odięta, chyba by się wprzód to przed Dozorcą Mieyscowym rozprawił, i dowiódł że Włościanin obowiązkom swoim zadosyć nie czyni.

7mo. Któryby Podstarości Ekonom lub Kommisarz wykroczył przeciw ninieyszemu Urządzeniu, i czyniłby iakie uciążliwości Ludowi, taki ma bydź wzięty przed Kommisyę ftawiony, i do Sądu Kryminalnego odany.

8vo. Gdyby Dziedzice czego się nie spodziewam, nakazywali lub popełniali podobne uciski isko przeciwni Celowi Powstania do odpowiedzi pociągnieni będą.

9no. Ważiennie Lud Wierzchni doznaiąc Sprawiedliwości i dobroci Rządu, powinien pozostałe dni Pańszczyzny odbywać, Zwierchności swoiey bydź posłusznym, gospodarstwapilnować, role dobre uprawiać i zasiewać, a gdy takowa ulga uczyniona iest dla Włościan z pobudek ratunku Oyczyzny, i Właściciele przez miłość Oyczyzny chętnie ią przyimuią, przeto Włościanie nie maią się wymawiać od naymów potrzebnych Dworom za przyzwoitą zapłatą.

10mo. Dla łatwieyszego dopilnowania porządku i zapewnienia co do skutku tych Zaleceń, podzielą Kommisye Porządkowe iak iest rzeczono w ich Organizacyi Woiewodztwa albo Ziemie lub Powiaty swoie na Dozory tak, żeby każdy Dozor Tysiąc a naywięcey Tysiąc Dwieście Gospodarzy Mieszkańców obeymował. Nadadzą tym Dozorcom naswiska od głowney Wsi lub Miasteczka, w takim zamkną ich okręgu, żeby łatwa Kommunikacya bydź mogła.

11mo. W każdym Dozorze wyznacza Dozorcę Człowieka zdatnego i poczciwego, który przez włożonych na siebie obowiązków w organizacyi Kommisyy Porządkowych będzie odbierał skargi od Ludu w iego uciskach, i od Dworu, w przypadku nieposłuszeństwa lub niesforności Ludu. Powinnością iego będzie rozsądzać spory, a gdyby Strony nie były kontente, do Kommisyi Porządkowey ie odsyłać.

12mo. Dobrodzieystwo Rządu w ulżeniu Ludowi ciężarów, zachęcić go powinno bardziey ieszcze do Rolnictwa, do obrony Oyczyzny. Gdyby więc hultaie iacy na się używaiąc dobroci i sprawiedliwości Rządu odwodzili Lud od pracy, buntowali przeciwko Dziedzicom, odmawiali od obrony Oyczyzny, Kommisye Porządkowe w swoich Woiewodztwach i Powiatach pilne na to mieć będą oko, i natychmiast takowych hultaiów łapać rozkażą i do Sądu Kryminalnego oddadzą. Nie mniey Kommisye Porządkowe czuwać maią nad włoczęgami którzyby w tym czasie Domy porzucali i po Kraiu włoczyli się, wszystkich takowych Ludzi chwytać i do wydziału bespieczeństwa w każdey Kommisyi będącego oddawać trzeba, a po zrobionym Examinie gdy się tułaczami i próżniakami okażą, do robot publicznych używać.

13mo. Duchowni naybliżsi Ludu Nauczyciele powinni mu przekładać iakie ma obowiązki dla Oyczyzny, która iest prawdziwa Matką względem niego okazuie. Ci Duchowni oświecać Lud powinni, że pracuiąc pilnie koło roli swoiey i Dworskiey równie miłą czyni Oyczyznie Offiarę, iak ten który ią orężem od zdzierstw i rabunkow żołnierstwa nieprzyiacielskiego zasłania, że pełniąc powinność względem Dworów zwłaszcza tak sfolgowaną przez ninieysze Urządzenie nic innego nie czyni, tylko winny dług wypłaca Dziedzicom od których grunta trzyma.

14to. Duchowni oboyga Obrządków ninieysze Urządzenie ogłaszać będą z Ambon po Kościołach i Cerkwiach ciągle przez Niedziel cztery. Procz tego Kommisye Porządkowe z grona swego lub z Obywatelów gorliwych o dobro Oyczyzny wyznaczą Osoby które obieżdżać będą Gromady po Wsiach i Parafiach, i onym toż Urządzenie głośno czytać i zachęcać będą aby w wdzięczni tak wielkiego dobrodzieystwa Rzeczypospolitey szczerą ochotą w iey obronie wypłacali się. Dan w Obozie pod Połańcem dnia 7 Maia 1794 Roku.

T. KOSCIUSZKO.

Zgodność z Oryginałem zaświadczam. Mecirzewski
Kommissarz Porząd. Woiew. Krak piora trzymaiący.

Uniwersał Urządzaiący powinności gruntowe Włościan i zapewniaiący dla nich skuteczną Opiekę Rządową bespieczeństwo Własności i Sprawiedliwość w Kommisyach Porządkowych.

Aleksander Orłowski, the author of numerous drawings and sketches depicting the insurrectionist struggle (compare reproductions on pp. 216 and 217), could be called the chronicler of the war of 1794. He also recorded many scenes of daily life in the insurrectionist camp. Here are several such sketches either done on the spot (e.g. scythebearers) or worked out in later years. They combine a chronicler's concern for the truth with artistic perfection. At times (e.g. the scene portraying Kosciuszko's soldiers in an inn or the sketch of the scythebearers) the artist's satirical bent is quite apparent

When word of the victory of Racławice was received, an uprising, long in the planning stage, broke out in Warsaw on 17 April 1794. Within two days Poland's capital was liberated, and Tsarist garrisons were forced to leave the city which now eagerly awaited Kosciuszko's arrival. The hero of the Warsaw insurrection was the shoemaker Jan Kiliński, a leader of the burghers who had distinguished themselves in the street skirmishes. His likeness is seen in a contemporary miniature: next to it is a military decoration bearing the date of the outbreak of the insurrection in Warsaw. A skirmish in Krakowskie Przedmieście in front of the Holy Cross Church was recorded by an eye-witness in the person of Jean-Pierre Norblin, a French painter who spent a great deal of time in Poland during that period

232

During the Kosciuszko Insurrection there arose in Warsaw a plebeian movement in favor of more radical change. In the streets of Warsaw there even appeared a gallows, on which several traitors were hanged. At times representatives of the Targowica camp, who were considered to be traitors to the homeland, were hanged in effigy. These revolutionary scenes were recorded by Norblin, while his pupil, Orłowski left behind some extremely interesting sketches of the Warsaw people participating in the struggle for the capital's independence

The culmination of the insurrection came with the siege of Warsaw by the combined forces of Russia and Prussia. Between 13 July and 6 September 1794 Kosciuszko supervised the town's defense, planning the construction of fortifications, arming and equipping his troops and personally commanding operations in the most difficult sectors. The defense of Warsaw against an army of 40,000 men, finally forcing the enemy to retreat, was considered the main victory of the insurrection's commander-in-chief. The letters of the Commander-in-chief to General Józef Orłowski (then Warsaw defense commandant, known to Kosciuszko from his days in the Corps of Cadets and subsequently in France) and to the mayor of insurrectionist Warsaw, Ignacy Wyssogota-Zakrzewski, reveal a feverish atmosphere of preparation for battle. In the letter to the mayor, who (like his worthy successor of a century and a half later, Stefan Starzyński) had organized the civilian defense of the capital, Kosciuszko revealed how much importance he attached to the participation of the townsmen as volunteers in the struggle

236

Zakrzeski kochany dziś przededniem zapewne będziemy attakowani a za tym proszę i żakli nam na miełoś Oyczyzny abyś piołowe dziś siła do Linij obywateli a gdy będą attakować aby wszyscy wyszli. Po wiedz mnie siedzy że styszałem że Obywatele niechą się do Lieyia, idzeli to prawda oddale go gdy z Oyczyzne nad wszysto przekładam Dnia 4 Septembra

Kosiuszko

Kosciuszko rewarded the military prowess of his soldiers with gold bands bearing the inscription: "The Fatherland to its Defender", the initials TK, the date 1794 and the award's serial number. The band pictured bears the number 28 and was presented by Kosciuszko to Capt. Józef Chłopicki who was later to become the leader of the November Insurrection

The Battle of Maciejowice, fought on 10 October 1794, marked the final chapter of the Kosciuszko Insurrection. In order to prevent fresh Russian reinforcements from joining up with an interventionist corps already engaged in combat with the Poles, Kosciuszko decided to bar their way with a hastily mustered army of 7,000 men under his personal command. In the course of extremely bitter fighting half of insurrectionists lost their lives and over 2,000 wounded were taken captive, and the battle ended in defeat for the Poles. The commander-in-chief himself was seriously wounded and was taken captive by the Russians. Three weeks later the Tsarist armies captured Warsaw, and five weeks after the ill-fated Battle of Maciejowice the insurrection was crushed. Both of the battle scenes presented here and the drawing of the wounded Kosciuszko being carried off the battlefield by Cossacks were the work of Jean-Pierre Norblin

The four-cornered military cap which, according to tradition, Kosciuszko wore in 1794, and a saber presented to him by his countrymen while he was in emigration in Paris

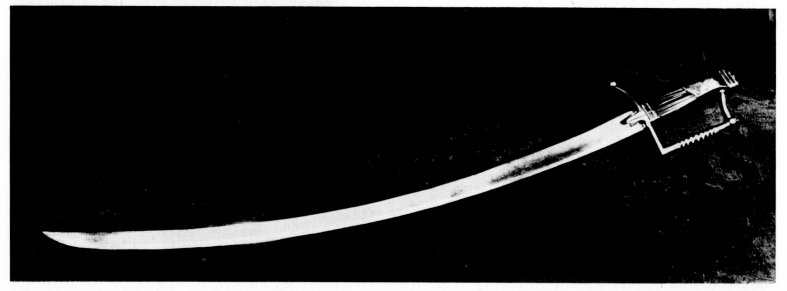

Chapter VI

In the Shadow of Defeat and the Glow of Legend

The siege of Savannah brought the heroic exploits of Casimir Pulaski to an abrupt end, whereas Maciejowice did not spell the doom of Thaddeus Kosciuszko, even though he apparently would have preferred it that way. Upon realizing the Poles' defeat, he had attempted to take his own life rather than fall into enemy hands, but his pistol failed to fire. Neither did the serious pike and saber wounds, inflicted on the fallen hero by a group of Cossacks, prove fatal. Fate still had 23 years of émigré life in store for Kosciuszko.

Some of Thaddeus Kosciuszko's biographers have referred to him as "a hero of 200 insurrectionist days", deeming his life prior to that period simply a prologue and calling the post-insurrection epilogue "the twilight of a hero". While it was indeed the insurrection that surrounded him with an heroic mystique, Kosciuszko had already gained fame during the war in defense of the Constitution of 3 May as the commander at the Battle of Dubienka. As a result, thanks to the support of the politicians, his candidacy for leadership of the future insurrection was put forward. Kościuszko was the object of a nationwide cult during the insurrection; the greatest and boldest of hopes had been placed in his leadership. The loss of the supreme commander consequently dealt a mortal blow to the uprising.

The collapse of the insurrection marked the end of Poland's independence. In 1795 the three neighboring powers incorporated what remained of the country's territory*. The abdication of King Stanislaus Augustus Poniatowski on 25 November 1795 was the last date in the history of the old royal Poland which was wiped off the map of Europe by the third partition. Nonetheless, the Polish nation remained; people who retained an awareness of Poland lived on. This truth was perhaps most eloquently expressed by Józef Wybicki, the author of a song which was to become the Polish national anthem: *Jeszcze Polska nie umarła, kiedy my żyjemy* ("Poland has not yet perished while we remain alive"). But before its strains were to resound in the ranks of a Polish army reactivated on Italian soil in 1797, the enemies of Poland would eagerly reiterate the words *Finis Poloniae,* allegedly uttered by Kosciuszko.

In reality Thaddeus Kosciuszko never said any such thing, although a Prussian newspaper reported that detail in its account of the Battle of Ma-

---

* See map on page 182

ciejowice. That bit of fallacious information, however, was widely propagated and made its way not only into tradition but also into the awareness of certain historians. Only in the 20th century was it disproved. The circumstances in which Kosciuszko (seriously wounded and unconscious) was taken captive rendered any utterance whatsoever impossible. Even if he was to have spoken those words in the split second before the Cossack lances reached him, it is highly unlikely that the sole witnesses of that episode — simple Cossacks — would have been able to pass on later that Latin exclamation to others. Be that as it may, the words *Finis Poloniae*, fabricated and subsequently eagerly bandied about especially by the Germans, were not without historical significance. The Prussian newspaper which first reported that occurrence in effect reflected the opinion not only of the partitioning powers but also of all of 19th century Europe which believed the Polish question to be closed once and for all. To the Poles, however, the collapse of the insurrection was tantamount to the collapse of Polish statehood, but never implied the end of Poland as such.

The great flash of hope that the tide of Poland's destiny could be stemmed and the great outburst of patriotic feeling that lasted throughout the insurrection — had subsided. Polish morale declined as the entire nation went into mourning. The nation's leader was in a St. Petersburg prison, thousands of former insurrectionists had been deported into the depths of Russia or forced into a lonely exile existence in Western Europe, and the population of Poland was now under foreign rule. Kosciuszko, who had symbolized the rebirth of his homeland throughout the insurrection, now exemplified its oppression. The hero had become a martyr.

The life of Thaddeus Kosciuszko after the ill-fated Battle of Maciejowice was a period of personal defeat which he painfully experienced both physically and mentally. He was never to return to his former vitality. Despite periods of heightened activity, his introversion and sense of alienation persisted.

The state of depression into which he fell as a captive might have explained this situation, although his mental health during his imprisonment at St. Petersburg is not easy to decipher. Whether the paresis of his lower extremities and resultant inability to walk stemmed from his battle wounds or whether his lameness was feigned — has never been conclusively determined.

At one point during his imprisonment at St. Petersburg Kosciuszko fell into such a state of apathy and melancholy that he stopped eating. Concerned about the prisoner's health, Catherine ordered him moved from the Petropavlovsk Fortress to the Marble Palace where he was afforded the best of medical care. Catherine needed Kosciuszko in order to keep the Prussians in check, as Russo-Prussian relations had grown tense in the interim.

The fate of Kosciuszko and other insurrectionists deported to Russia changed considerably with the ascent of Paul I to the imperial throne. In order to demonstrate the difference in his policy from that of his mother the tsarina, the new tsar was prepared to pardon all the insurrectionists imprisoned by her on condition that Kosciuszko would take an obsequious oath. At a personal meeting with the tsar (November 1796) Kosciuszko accepted this proposal, pledging to return to America, his "second homeland", rather than to partitioned Poland. Thus he voluntarily condemned himself to banishment rather than remain under the tsar's authority, presumably convinced that that would lead to further humiliation owing to his declaration of loyalty. For many years that oath was to torment Kosciuszko, for even though it was taken *pro publico bono*, it signified moral capitulation.

In December 1796 Thaddeus Kosciuszko left St. Petersburg in the company of two comrades. The first was Julian Ursyn Niemcewicz, an outstanding writer and political thinker who had served as his secretary during the insurrection and later had been a fellow prisoner at St. Petersburg. The second was a husky young officer. The latter took good care of Kosciuszko and carried him whenever necessary, since the reconvalescent was unable to move about on his own. The journey led them via Finland and Sweden, where they stayed several months, to England. Kosciuszko was heartily welcomed everywhere he went and called "a martyr of freedom". His appearance could only elicit sympathy. The portraits of him painted at Stockholm and London depicted an ailing Kosciuszko lying on a sofa, with a bandage on his still unhealed head wound.

Despite his ill health, Kosciuszko did not postpone his journey to the United States. In June 1797 he set forth on a wearisome, two-month-long voyage across the Atlantic and arrived at Philadelphia, as he had done once before. The inhabitants of that town welcomed Kosciuszko with the highest esteem. The wildly cheering crowd unharnessed the horses of his carriage and themselves drew the Polish visitor through the streets of Philadelphia at the head of a triumphant procession. By contrast, among American ruling circles, which had moved away from the republican ideals of their predecessors, the visit was not a source of satisfaction. The only representative of official circles with whom Kosciuszko renewed his friendship and established close ties was Thomas Jefferson, a true republican who was then vice-president (and was later to become president) of the United States. This friendship was to last until Kosciuszko's death. The two corresponded with each other, and Kosciuszko named Jefferson the administrator of his American estate. In it he instructed his friend to use the payments owed him by the American government for the purchase, liberation and education of Negro slaves.

Kosciuszko's life in America was one of quiet seclusion. He would meet with former comrades-in-arms, and was respected and honored as a fighter for the cause of liberty. He spent most of his time in his modest residence in Philadelphia, still unable to walk unassisted. And then, what had all the markings of a peaceful life-long sojourn in his second homeland was cut short by a decision to return to Europe, a bare nine months after his departure. This change of heart was presumably the result of a French pledge which unfolded before Kosciuszko the prospect of playing at the side of France a role of no mean importance to the Polish cause.

In May 1798 quite unexpectedly Kosciuszko left the United States under the assumed name of Baron Thomas Kannberg. He had informed his closest comrade, Niemcewicz, of this only a few hours before his departure. One sensational aspect of this decision was the fact that once he set foot on board ship he suddenly "forgot" about the lameness which impeded his walking and would never experience such ailments again. This and other details have inclined some historians to theorize that from the outset of his reconvalescence, beginning with his being taken to Russia, Kosciuszko had deliberately sought to create the impression that he was crippled. His caution and suspicious nature, which had bordered on the pathological during his St. Petersburg period, bade him to continue the deception until he found himself en route to France under the guise of Baron Kannberg, fired by the hope of reversing his destiny.

Upon setting foot on French soil Kosciuszko became the object of what appeared to be great interest on the part of the Directorate. It soon turned out, however, that no concrete proposals awaited him. French diplomacy had decided to use him in its power play with Prussia in order to facilitate the conclusion of a Franco-Prussian alliance. For the sake of appearances, however, the deception was kept up for a time. But in reality the situation was much like that in which Kosciuszko found himself in St. Petersburg, when Catherine II had attempted to use him as a trump card against Prussia.

At the same time Kosciuszko established closer ties with the Polish Legions, formed in Italy under the command of General Jan Henryk Dąbrowski, his erstwhile subordinate during the insurrection. The legionaries, who had thrown in their lot with France, wanted Kosciuszko to assume command of the Polish troops that would fight for Poland's liberation under French banners. Kosciuszko declined, as he did not believe this was the right road to independence. He also did not believe in the opportunity created for Poland in 1806 by Napoleon's war against Prussia. Since Napoleon failed to give any concrete pledges concerning Poland's future, he refused to lend his personal authority to the recruitment of a Polish army to be formed on the liberated lands of the Prussian partition. The history of the Duchy of Warsaw which Napoleon created does not include the name of Thaddeus Kosciuszko who stood apart from this new stage in the struggle for Polish independence. By that time the 60-year-old Kosciuszko was but a symbol of the past.

And yet, despite his aloofness which was presumably rooted in distrust of the French emperor for the latter's betrayal of republican ideals, Kosciuszko never ceased to contemplate the future liberation of the Homeland. The last testament of Kosciuszko the national leader was a pamphlet written in 1800 entitled *Are the Poles Capable of Winning Independence?* Although the actual author was his Paris secretary, the Polish Jacobin Józef Pawlikowski, the pamphlet contained the views of Kosciuszko. It emanates a faith in the unquenchable vitality of the nation, which must achieve its independence on its own, and expresses scepticism about the efficacy of foreign assistance. This is amply illustrated by the following excerpt:

"The nation yearning for independence needs to have confidence in its own forces. If it is devoid of that sentiment, if it seeks to uphold its existence not through its own efforts but through foreign support or favor, then one may safely assume that it will achieve neither happiness, nor virtue nor glory."

Thaddeus Kosciuszko would once again attempt to use his authority to promote the Polish cause when he met with Tsar Alexander I after the defeat of Napoleon. The tsar made far-reaching promises concerning the happy future of the Kingdom of Poland which had arisen under his scepter in place of the Napoleonic Duchy of Warsaw. Therein Kosciuszko saw the potential nucleus for a reborn Polish state. Such hopes were dashed two years later at the Congress of Vienna. In 1815 the then 69-year-old Kosciuszko traveled in all haste from Paris to Vienna to induce Tsar Alexander to make good on his promises. But all his efforts proved futile, thereby reaffirming Kosciuszko's own words that independence could not be regained through foreign support or favor.

Kosciuszko spent the last two years of his life at Solothurn in Switzerland, living with a Swiss family called Zeltner. Occasionally Polish émigrés passing through Switzerland would visit him. He also carried on a correspondence with people in Poland. In one letter to Prince Adam Jerzy Czartoryski, the tsar's advisor on Polish affairs, Kosciuszko wrote at length on the peasant question. In the name of social justice and the country's economic development he urged the prince to provide for the needs of the neglected and oppressed peasantry. That letter of 19 July 1815, known as "the civic testament of Kosciuszko", concluded with the words:

"All true Poles who link their personal interests with those of the nation are unanimously in favor of such measures towards the peasantry so that in time they might be liberated from serfdom and granted ownership of their land. I appeal to all sublime, noble and humane souls — and such are you all, my Countrymen. Set a date in advance. Dare I hope that within 20 years all would be free and affranchised? Great God, what an epoch of universal joy and national prosperity that would be! Look into your hearts once more and be just."

As the above clearly indicates, the slogans of freedom and equality were to guide Kosciuszko's thinking right up to the end. He died at Solothurn on 15 October 1817 without a single countryman at his death-bed. Kosciuszko's death caused widespread reverberations in Poland and many other countries as well. On 20 January 1818 William H. Harrison (later president of the United States) said in an address to Congress:

"Kosciuszko, the martyr of liberty, is no more! In analysing the life of that great man we can see a steadfastness of character all the more admirable since it is so rarely encountered. He was not the friend of mankind on one occasion, only to become its oppressor on the next; throughout his life he upheld his noble principles which had set him apart in his youth when he left his country and those near and dear to him in order to fight for human rights in another hemisphere. ... His fame will last as long as freedom reigns throughout the world; as long as defenders of freedom will give up their lives at the altar of freedom, the name of Kosciuszko will dwell amongst us."

The Poles decided to bring Kosciuszko's mortal remains to Poland and lay them to rest in the national pantheon, among the crypts of Poland's monarchs at Wawel Castle in Cracow. The funeral ceremony, which took place in June 1818, was a great patriotic manifestation. The townspeople of Cracow, where Kosciuszko had experienced the greatest day of his life in taking the oath as Supreme Commander, bade farewell to their leader for the last time and surrounded him with legend. That tribute was symbolized by the huge mound raised in honor of Kosciuszko in Cracow in keeping with ancient Slavonic custom.

He had already gained fame during his lifetime. The legend of his exploits at Dubienka paved his way to leadership of the insurrection. The legend of the victor of Racławice instilled hope in the Poles in the days of the insurrection that he would indeed "sever the fetters in which the nation groaned". After Maciejowice the star of the Supreme Commander began to wane, and no more was heard of his legend until after his death, when it blossomed forth in all its glory to inspire succeeding generations seeking roads to the independence of the fatherland.

In him they would see a man for whom the affairs of the nation constituted the highest good; they would see somebody willing to give his all for the cause of freedom, somebody who stood at the nation's helm in order to alter its lot by linking the question of independence with the revolutionary ideal of "universal happiness." The lack of such a man was to be painfully felt during subsequent Polish insurrections, whose weak and indecisive leadership, absence of a socio-political program and failure to appreciate the necessity of involving all classes of the nation in the struggle would serve to diminish the chance of victory. For that very reason the years of subjugation would time and again rekindle the memory of the legendary "hero of Racławice" who truly led the entire nation towards the goal of "freedom, integrity and independence".

Legends generally remain alive especially when they affect issues of continuing relevance. So it was with the Kosciuszko legend which developed during the period of foreign domination as a symbol of the Polish nation's quest for independence. Another, parallel strain of that legend was the drive towards social reform which saw in Kosciuszko a patron of the cause of liberating the peasantry. Both those strains went to form a vital part of Polish history over two centuries, and for that reason the leader of the first Polish nationwide insurrection continued to occupy such a prominent place in the hierarchy of national and social awareness.

Be that as it may, Kosciuszko had not succeeded in achieving what he had hoped. The Kosciuszkian epic had lasted only 200 days. During that time his only major military success was the effective defense of Warsaw. The insurrection was ultimately quelled. Kosciuszko suffered a shattering defeat both as the leader of the insurrection and as military commander at the Battle of Maciejowice. All that might have led to negative appraisals, and in fact there were and still are many controversies about Kosciuszko's military and political abilities among historians. What has remained beyond question is his fidelity to the republican ideal for which he fought on the other side of the Atlantic, which he served in defending the Constitution of 3 May and for which he took command of the insurrection. In the general consciousness of the Poles Kosciuszko, whose popularity has surpassed that of any other historical figure, continues to represent the ideals of the freedom and brotherhood of peoples — ideals which have lost none of the luster they had 200 years ago.

Such is the legend of Kosciuszko, the heroic commander of Racławice, the "martyr of freedom" in exile, and above all the "friend of mankind" who believed in, fought for and remained ever faithful to the freedom of peoples and universal happiness.

How does the Pulaski legend compare with this? Death on the field of battle frequently gives rise to heroic legends, for it interrupts the record at the most favorable point, absolves the hero of the necessity of continuing to prove himself before history and often eclipses what has transpired in his earlier life.

Casimir Pulaski fell in glory on the day of battle and has gone down in history as "the hero of Savannah". That same Pulaski, whose Legion had not enjoyed the trust of Congress, who had been accused of making too free with the money meant for his unit and who, in his final letter to Congress, had complained: "Why is it that you have so little confidence in me?" — was now beyond the reach of such mundane reproofs. When the ship on which Pulaski had died reached Charleston, an extremely solemn, symbolic funeral with full military honors was held in his memory. And when Congress, with which he had never been able to find a common language, learnt of his death, it decided to raise a monument in this honor.

Well over a century later when the monument to Pulaski was unveiled at Washington, the President of the United States, William Taft, said: "He was a knight to the core, the son of a knightly nation, and knightly in attitude and habits; manly, undaunted, courageous, bold — though with a feminine gentleness and politeness — and mild in manner was he whose name combines all the charm and romanticism of former chivalry".

That sketch undoubtedly contains much truth, although it does not provide a complete image. The other side of the coin — maladjustment to American society, and a difficult and irascible personality intolerant of higher authority — was conveniently overlooked. Were it not for his supreme sacrifice, in all certainty General Pulaski would not have occupied a position in the American pantheon. Perhaps all that would have remained was the image of him expressed in his initial period of service by George Washington, one of the Americans most favorably disposed towards Pulaski; "Beyond the slightest doubt he is a most active and courageous gentleman; but he lacks the more intimate knowledge of our language and customs needed to make him a valuable officer."

In Poland the legend of "the most famous leader of the confederation" had already begun to grow up around Pulaski during his confederate involvement. It became somewhat tarnished by his part in a plot to abduct the king which, in spite of everything, in the world of that period smacked of a scandal. The stigma of "regicide" was not removed until 14 years after his death. As a result of the untiring efforts of his last living brother, Antoni, the parliamentary verdict of 1773, condemning the "ignominious Pulaski" to death, was annulled in 1793. To later generations his involvement in a plot against a king, who in time was held to have had a share of responsibility for the tragedy of the partitions, ceased to be disgraceful. Thus Casimir Pulaski, "the defender of Jasna Góra", was included in the chronicles of post-partition Poland as the one who first rose in defense of Poland's sovereignty when it was threatened by tsarist Russia. To this very day historians dispute the political sense of unleashing the confederate war which led directly to the first partition of Poland. But their allegations, leveled at the errors of the political leadership, have not sought to denigrate the honorable role that the most famous Bar partisan, Casimir Pulaski, played both in that and later struggles.

To future generations of Poles, who on more than one occasion would again engage in partisan-style uprisings, Pulaski became a model of courage and daring, of endurance and relentlessness in battling against overwhelming odds. The uniqueness of Pulaski's "chivalrous romanticism" is what seems to strike the Americans most. To the Poles, however, that characteristic was by no means considered unique; on the contrary, a "true Pole" and a "true soldier" must be the personification of precisely those traits that Pulaski possessed. Hence the "Pulaski legend" has remained so close to Polish hearts. His countrymen have found in him the all but ideal model of a true soldier-patriot.

It is difficult to compare the historical status of Thaddeus Kosciuszko and Casimir Pulaski.

To his countrymen Kosciuszko will always remain a standard-bearer, a national leader and ideologist while Pulaski is regarded as the embodiment of soldierly virtues. It was their common involvement in the American War of Independence that elevated them to similar rank. Both of them were forerunners of the Polish tradition of struggle "for your freedom and ours" which arose half a century later during the November Insurrection (1830—31). As a result, both the heroes of this book — Kosciuszko and Pulaski — have been accorded a worthy place in the history of the struggle for the freedom and independence of nations.

There are numerous examples of the unfading popularity of Thaddeus Kosciuszko and Casimir Pulaski, ranging from localities, streets and ships named after them to postage stamps bearing their likenesses. Schools, factories and military formations have chosen them as their patrons. Monuments have been erected to them and books about their lives have been written. All those gestures serve to reaffirm our belief in the noble ideals for which they stood. By honoring the heroes of this book, we also honor the ideals of freedom and independence, patriotism and brotherhood.

In the figure of Thaddeus Kosciuszko these ideals found a particularly clear reflection. This is due not only to the stature of the leader of the uprising which has gone down in history as the Kosciuszko insurrection, but also to the wide echoes it awakened in Poland and the whole world. The national nature of the uprising gave it something of a precursory character and made Thaddeus Kosciuszko symbol of a new age.

"The Leader in peasant garb" — the most popular, and frequently reproduced portrait of Thaddeus Kosciuszko — is a symbol of Republican democracy, indicative of the desire to ensure happiness and success to all mankind. This idea was expressed by Kosciuszko at Racławice, when he declared: "I shall always pay close heed to the voice and the needs of the people. The reason I took up arms was that I wanted to see the inhabitants of all the Polish lands genuinely happy."

When 150 years after the insurrection, in 1944, People's Poland was born, Thaddeus Kosciuszko, of all Polish historical figures, seemed to be closest to the new Poland. In 1943 his name was written on the battle standard of the brigade which had just been formed in the Soviet Union and which was to be the nucleus of the Polish People's Army. An occasion for the whole nation to honor the memory of the author of the Połaniec Proclamation was afforded by the 200th anniversary of his birth, which was celebrated in 1946, and the 150th anniversary of his death, which fell in 1967. When on the occasion of the 1000th anniversary of the founding of the Polish state Poles from all walks of life were canvassed for their opinions, it turned out that of all Poland's national heroes, Kosciuszko was the most known and loved. Thus in recent times too the Kosciuszko legend has taken on new luster.

Kosciuszko's contemporaries saw in him a man destined to become a legendary figure; this is indicated by some of the portraits of Kosciuszko done during his lifetime which endowed the commander of Racławice with heroic attributes. This may be said of the beautiful cameo carved in carnelian by Jan Regulski; the artist portrayed Kosciuszko in a Corinthian helmet and included against the background of an ancient shield crossed scythes and lances, one of which is crowned with a "Phrygian cap"

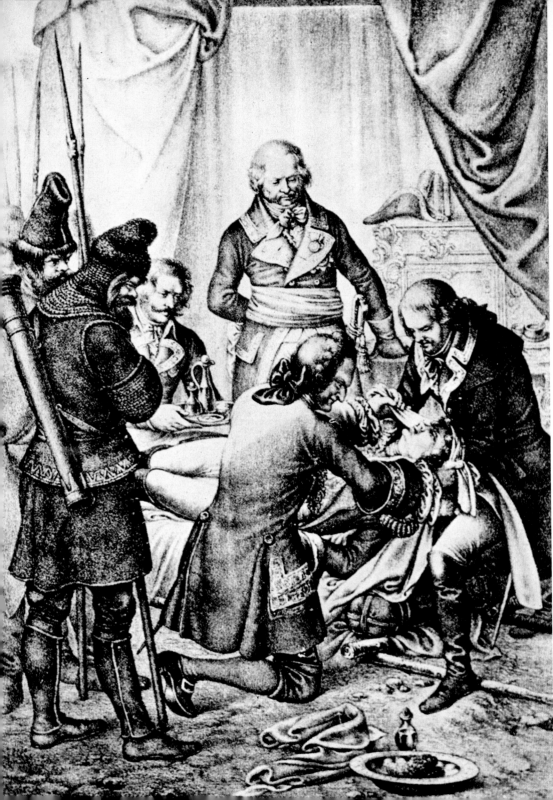

The legend of the "savior of the homeland" gave way on the battlefield of Maciejowice to the legend of the "martyr of freedom". Two hundred days after the outbreak of the insurrection the struggle of the leader, whose authority, unswerving adamancy and dedication to the cause had bolstered the Poles' will to fight, came to an end. He was seriously wounded on the field of battle and taken captive while unconscious. This 19th-century lithograph portrays the dressing of Kosciuszko's wounds at the quarters of General Fersen, the commander of the Russian corps

254

From Maciejowice Kosciuszko was transported to St Petersburg where he was imprisoned for two years. After the death of Catherine II, the new Tsar, Paul I, had him released. The copper engravings shown here depict a visit paid by the tsar in November 1796 to the Marble Palace at St Petersburg, where Kosciuszko spent most of his confinement, and Kosciuszko's visit to the tsar's Winter Palace. This latter scene, which also portrays other Poles released from captivity, is of a strictly symbolic nature, as the tsar's meetings with Kosciuszko took place without such a large entourage

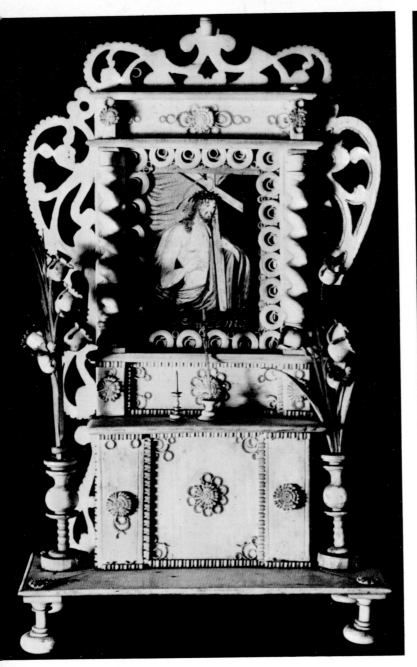

Thaddeus Kosciuszko, whose health during his confinement at St Petersburg returned very slowly (he also experienced serious inner crises), filled his time practicing various artistic handicrafts. Pictured are several objects made by him at that time: a miniature altar and shrine of wood and papier mâché, a decorative casket and a sugar-bowl fashioned from a coconut shell

THADDEUS KOSCIUSKO,
Polſk Fältherre.

Libertas Animae Deo, Corporis Paulo Petri Filio.

On 19 December 1796 Kosciuszko left St Petersburg and via Finland and Sweden traveled to England, whence he made his way to America, his "second homeland". Several portraits of the "martyr of freedom" were produced at that time in Sweden and England. They depict a figure enfeebled by war wounds and imprisonment with a bandage covering a still unhealed head wound. Kosciuszko was unable to walk unassisted during that period.

According to Julian Ursyn Niemcewicz, Kosciuszko's adjutant and close personal friend, the oil portrait painted by the English artist Richard Cosway in London (1797) "bore a remarkable resemblance", even though it must have been sketched surreptitiously, as Kosciuszko refused to pose for painters.

Six months after leaving St Petersburg Kosciuszko set sail for America from Bristol. A modest plaque now commemorates Kosciuszko's sojourn in that town

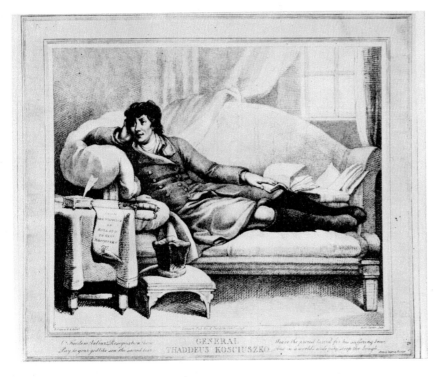

GENERAL
THADDEUS KOSCIUSZKO

THE POLISH PATRIOT
KOSCIUSZKO
STAYED HERE JUNE 1797

Public Law 92-524
92nd Congress, S. 1973
October 21, 1972

An Act

86 STAT. 1046

To provide for the establishment of the Thaddeus Kosciuszko Home National Historic Site in the State of Pennsylvania, and for other purposes.

Be it enacted by the Senate and House of Representatives of the United States of America in Congress assembled, That, in order to provide for the development of a suitable memorial to General Thaddeus Kosciuszko, great Polish patriot and hero of the American Revolution, the Secretary of the Interior is authorized to acquire by donation or purchase with donated funds the property at the northwest corner of Third and Pine Streets specifically designated as 301 Pine Street and/or 342 South Third Street, Philadelphia, Pennsylvania, including improvements thereon, together with such adjacent land and interests therein as the Secretary may deem necessary for the establishment and administration of the property as a national memorial.

Thaddeus Kosciuszko Home National Historic Site, Pa. Establishment. Land acquisition.

SEC. 2. The property acquired pursuant to the first section of this Act shall be known as the Thaddeus Kosciuszko National Memorial and it shall be administered by the Secretary of the Interior in accordance with the Act of August 25, 1916 (39 Stat. 535), as amended and supplemented (16 U.S.C. 1, 2-4), and the Act of August 21, 1935 (49 Stat. 666; 16 U.S.C. 461-467).

Administration.

SEC. 3. There are hereby authorized to be appropriated not more than $592,000 for the development of the national memorial.

Appropriation.

Approved October 21, 1972.

On 18 August 1797 Kosciuszko arrived in Philadelphia. The house in which he lived — thanks to the efforts of Edward Piszek, who is known for his services to the American Polish community — upon restoration, is to become the Kosciuszko Museum. The photograph shows the building at 301 Pine Street, Philadelphia, prior to restauration.

Alongside is a photocopy of the act of Congress, passed on 21 October 1972, proclaiming the Kosciuszko house at Philadelphia a national historic site.

Several small mementoes of Kosciuszko's second sojourn in the United States (August 1797 — May 1798) have survived. They include a portrait of a young girl (Kosciuszko is said to have sketched many such portraits at that time), a letter of courtesy to a Philadelphia publicist and a commemorative saber sent from England as a gift for Kosciuszko

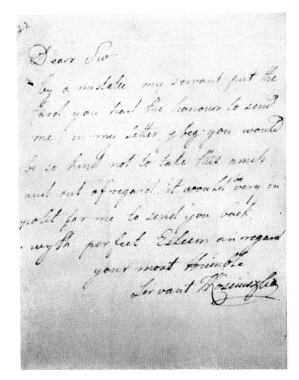

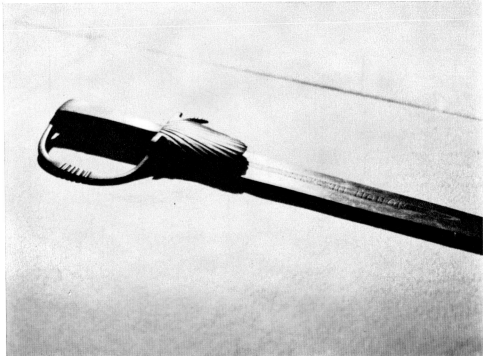

Thomas Jefferson

A Philosopher a Patriot and a Friend

Dessiné par son Ami Tadée Kosciuszko

Et Gravé par Mr. Sokolnicki

Thomas Jefferson, then vice-president of the United States, was the only person to establish close ties with Kosciuszko during the latter's second stay in America. Jefferson continued to espouse truly republican views at a time when most American politicians had moved away from the democratic ideals prevalent during the War of Independence. A token of that friendship is a portrait of Jefferson painted, according to the inscription, by "his friend, Thaddeus Kosciuszko". The solicitude which Jefferson showed for Kosciuszko may be illustrated by the letter sent to the secretary of the treasury in 1814. In it Jefferson described Kosciuszko's difficult financial plight and pointed out that he had not even received any interest on the sum owed him by the American government. He also asserted that Kosciuszko's service to the American revolution and his undying dedication to the cause of liberty made him particularly dear to the heart of America

Dear Sir   Monticello May 8. 14.

Genl. Kosciuszko whose revolutionary services and general devotion
to the cause of liberty have rendered him dear to this country, made a depo-
sit of all his funds in the monied institutions of this country, placing them
under my general superintendance, which is exercised through mr Barnes
who will have the honor of handing you this letter, and whom I take this occasion to make known to you for his great worth. I have instructed him to
dispose of the General's bankstock and to invest it in the new loan of the
US. but the immediate object of this letter is to observe that during the war
we have found it impracticable to remit to the General his annual
interest, in consequence of which his letters inform me of his great
distress in Paris, which must I know be great indeed. I have supposed it
possible that he might perhaps be availed of some of the money
transactions of your department so as to recieve his remittances thro'
them. any facility you may be so kind as to offer to mr Barnes for
this purpose, besides being recieved as a personal favor to myself, will
extend a much needed relief to one of our great revolutionary worthies.

I avail myself of this first occasion of congratulating you on
your accession to the honorable and important station you now occupy.
it is always a gratification to me to see the public offices confided to
those whom I know to come into them with singleness of views to the
public good. Accept the assurance of my great respect & esteem.

The honble   Th:Jefferson
G. W. Campbell
    Secretary of the treasury.

When he left the United States in May 1798, Thaddeus Kosciuszko left behind a testament regarding the disposition of the sums owed him by the American government. It was a testimony to Kosciuszko's profound democratic convictions. The manuscript here reproduced is a rough draft of the testament, written by Kosciuszko in his somewhat broken English. On the basis of this draft Jefferson drew up the version which was later to become widely known. Worth citing, however, is Kosciuszko's original version, some of whose formulations are more direct and pointed:

"I beg Mr Jefferson that in case I should die without will or testament, he should bye out of my money so many Negroes and free them, that the restant Sum should be sufficient to give them education and provide for their maintenance. That is to say each should know before, the duty of a Cytyzen in the free Government, that he must defend his Country against foreign as well as internal Enemis who would wish to change the Constitution for the vorst to inslave them by degree afterwards, to have good and human heart sensible for the sufferings of others, each must be maried and have 100 ackres of land, wyth instruments, Cattle for tillage and know how to manage and Gouvern it as well to know how behave to neybourghs, always wyth kindness and ready to help them — to themselves frugal to their Children give good education. I mean as to the heart and the duty to their Country, in gratitude to me to make themselves happy as possible. T. Kosciuszko"

In addition to the back pay for his eight years of service in the army, the American government granted Kosciuszko a parcel of land in Ohio. An 1803 plan of that 500-acre parcel (of which he never took possession) has survived down to the present. To this very day the local populace refers to it as "Kosciuszko Land". The scenery of these parts is shown in the photograph

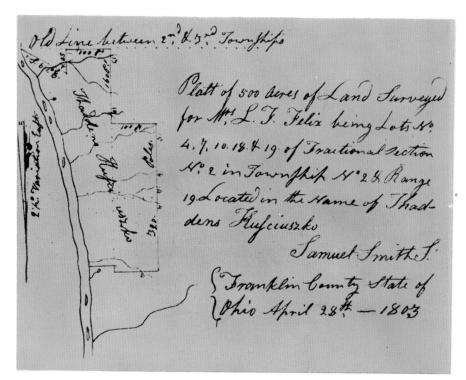

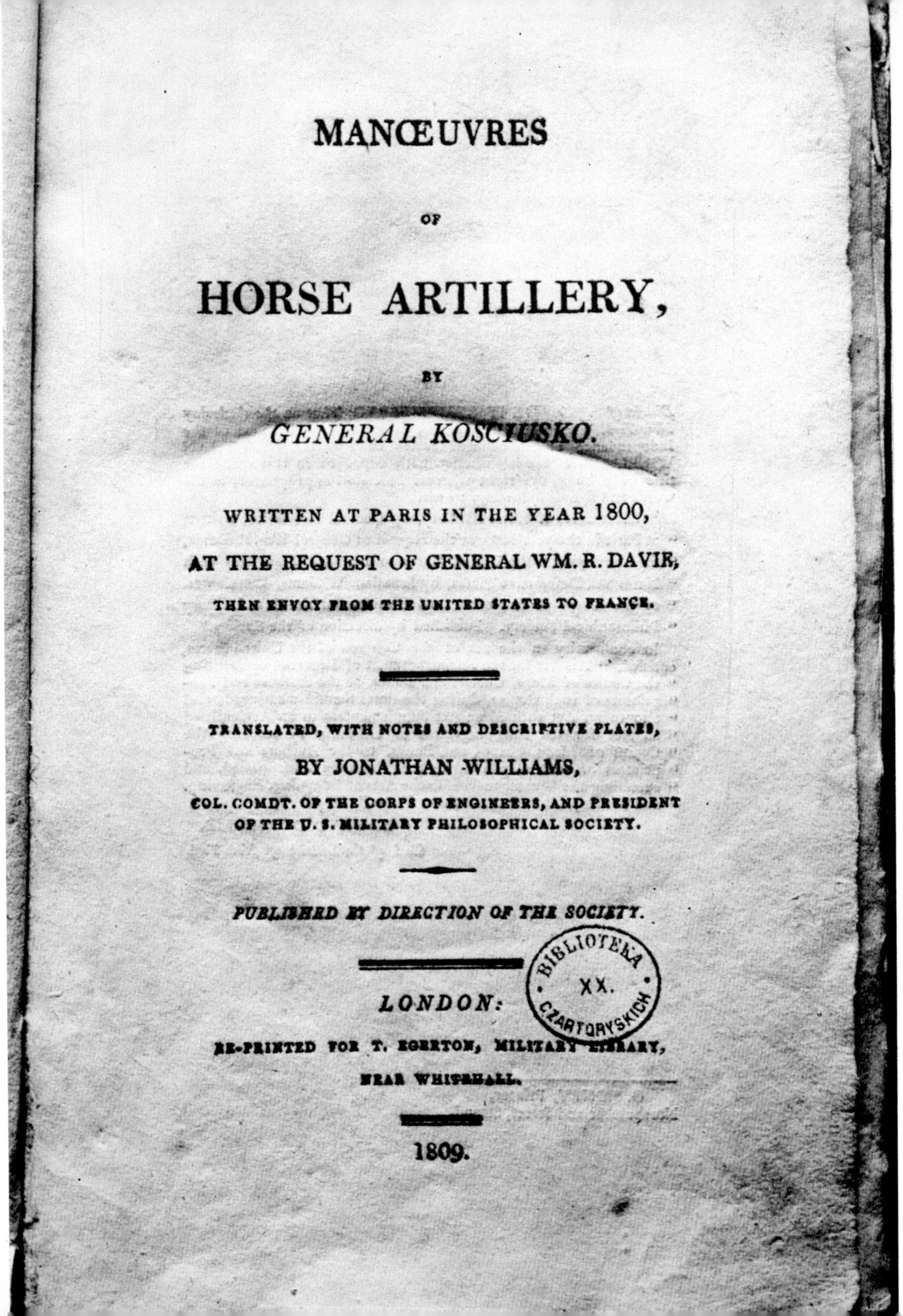

MANŒUVRES

OF

HORSE ARTILLERY,

BY

GENERAL KOSCIUSKO.

WRITTEN AT PARIS IN THE YEAR 1800,

AT THE REQUEST OF GENERAL WM. R. DAVIE,

THEN ENVOY FROM THE UNITED STATES TO FRANCE.

———

TRANSLATED, WITH NOTES AND DESCRIPTIVE PLATES,

BY JONATHAN WILLIAMS,

COL. COMDT. OF THE CORPS OF ENGINEERS, AND PRESIDENT
OF THE U. S. MILITARY PHILOSOPHICAL SOCIETY.

———

PUBLISHED BY DIRECTION OF THE SOCIETY.

LONDON:

RE-PRINTED FOR T. EGERTON, MILITARY LIBRARY,
NEAR WHITEHALL.

1809.

The book Manoeuvres of Horse Artillery, written by Kosciuszko in 1800 at the request of the American consul in Paris, attested to the Pole's continuing ties with America after his departure therefrom. It marked the first elaboration in military literature of the principles of horse artillery, a new branch of the armed forces (designed to provide support for cavalry), which had been introduced in various countries since the mid-18th century. Published in 1808 in the form of a manual, it was a standard work at American military academies for many years. Reproduced is a facsimile of the London edition. On the opposite page: a drawing by Jean-Pierre Norblin depicting Kosciuszko's artillery on the march and the barrel of a Polish cannon from the insurrection period. The inscription on the barrel states that the cannon, which was buried after the war of 1794, by peasants from Węglany in the Sandomierz region, was dug up again after the country's liberation in 1809 and presented to Gen. Dąbrowski

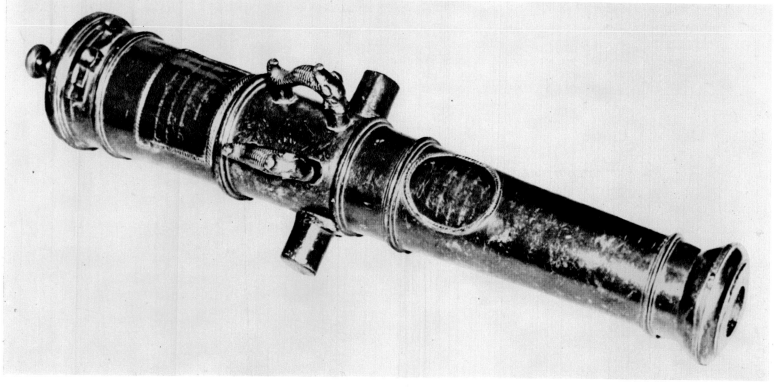

The partitioning powers sought to promote the view that the fall of the Kosciuszko Insurrection, followed by the third partition and the elimination of Poland from the map of Europe, meant the definitive end of the Polish state. For that reason the words "Finis Poloniae", which Thaddeus Kosciuszko was supposed to have said after the defeat at Maciejowice, were persistently repeated by the Prussians. This mid-19th-century German drawing depicts Kosciuszko falling from his steed and uttering those words which the artist included in the caption. This beautiful illustration was probably not inspired by anti-Polish sentiments, but it does indicate the extent to which the conviction that Maciejowice spelled the end of Polish statehood had taken root in the partitioning countries

«FINIS POLONIAE!»

Less than three years after the fall of the Kosciuszko Insurrection, the Polish Legions were formed in Italy. That force exemplified through its struggle the idea that "Poland has not yet perished". With those words began the "Hymn of the Legions", known as "Dąbrowski's Mazurka", which was written in 1797 by Józef Wybicki. It ended with the words: "Enough of this captivity! We have our Racławice scythes and Kosciuszko, the Lord willing."

The legionaries considered Kosciuszko their spiritual leader. He did not assume the command of the legions, however, as he did not trust Napoleon, but he did support their cause. Besides the letters and appeals which he sent to Polish soldiers and officers fighting in the legions, another extremely valuable memento has survived: a marble bust of Kosciuszko in the Roman tradition. Created by a Swiss sculptor, it was presented to Kosciuszko in Paris in 1800 by a group of Polish officers serving in Napoleon's army. The bust is inscribed with the words "He fought solely for the freedom and rights of man"

A miniature dating from 1794 and depicting Kosciuszko in a general's uniform saluting with his saber the insurrectionary army as it marches past

The dissertation entitled "Are the Poles Capable of Independence?" became the catechism of successive generations of Poles struggling for the liberation of their country from foreign subjugation. Written and published in 1800 in Paris, it contained the ideas of Thaddeus Kosciuszko set down in writing by Józef Pawlikowski, a radical young political activist close to Kosciuszko. During the 19th century this pamphlet went through seven editions. The leitmotiv of this patriotic testament was the conviction expressed in the introduction that "A nation desiring independence needs to have confidence in its own forces. If it lacks that sentiment, if it strives to uphold its existence not through its own efforts but through foreign support or favor, it may be boldly stated that it will achieve neither hapiness, nor virtue nor glory." Reproduced is a fragment of the final portion of the well-known pamphlet which served as an inspiration to later Polish insurrections

CZY POLACY

MOGĄ SIĘ WYBIĆ NA

NIEPODLEGŁOŚĆ?

POLACY! Pokazałem wam drogi do niepodległości. Nie wzbudzam w was szlachetnéj rozpaczy (już daliście jéj dowody) ale zachęcam do pewnych zwycięstw, gdy z odwagą rzucicie się na nieprzyjaciół. Macie wszystko do zwycięstw, odważcie się tylko zwyciężyć. Gdy mężnie *wszyscy* walczyć będziecie, nieprzyjaciel choćby był liczniéjszy jak jest teraz, nie potrafi was pokonać. Jeżeli zaś teraz nie pokruszycie jarzma, nie narzekajcie na niebo, bo *wy sami* autorami jesteście waszéj sromoty. Widzę w tém wymierzoną słuszność aby ci gnuśnieli w niewoli, którzy obojętném okiem patrzą na zdeptaną sprawiedliwość i ciśnioną ludzkość....

Kosciuszko did not believe that Poland could be liberated through Napoleon's assistance. Hence he remained on the sidelines even when Napoleon's army entered Polish territory in 1806. Less than a decade after the establishment of the Polish Legions in Italy, the words of their battle hymn had come true: the Polish soldier had finally made his way back to a liberated homeland. In November 1806 the creator of the Polish Legions, Gen. Jan Henryk Dąbrowski, marched into Poznań at the head of Polish troops. That scene was recorded by his contemporary, the painter Jan Gładysz. On the opposite page: a grenadier and a cavalryman of the Dąbrowski Legions

Legia polskie posiłkowe Lombardzkie
1797 - 1800.
Grenadyer.

Legia polska posiłkowa Lombardzka
Kawalerya
1799 - 1800.

273

Kosciuszko spent the final two years of his life at Solothurn, Switzerland, and was only occasionally visited by his
countrymen passing through. A year before his death the
English painter Richard R. Reinagle painted his portrait.
Below is a miniature based on that painting. Both likenesses of the then 70-year-old Kosciuszko appear somewhat
idealized. More true to life was the portrait painted by
Józef Peszka on the basis of a drawing by a Swiss friend
of Kosciuszko's. (Compare reproduction on p. 278)

Mementoes from the final years of Kosciuszko's life: an earthenware cup with a white glaze and bronze inscription "Boże day" ("Give us, O Lord"); a chess set and a wooden candlestick made by Kosciuszko which graced the mantle of his last abode; and a tortoise-shell-lined urn with the inscriptions: "Modesty", "Civic Virtue" and "Tranquility"

T. KOSCIUSZKO

The last likeness of Thaddeus Kosciuszko, a drawing produced two months before his death by his friend, X. Zeltner, at whose home he lived in Solothurn. Right: the symbolic tombstone of Thaddeus Kosciuszko in the cemetery at Zuchwyl near Solothurn (after a 19th-century Swiss lithograph) and a view of that site as it looks today

VISCERA TADEI
KOSCIUSKO
DEPOSITA DIE
XVII OCTOBRIS
MDCCCXVII.

Lith. de A. Merian à Basle.

Monument du GÉNÉRAL KOSCIUSKO à Zuchwyl

près de Soleure.

In 1818 the mortal remains of Thaddeus Kosciuszko were moved to Cracow, although his heart remained outside of Poland until 1927. In 1894 it was enshrined in the castle chapel at Rapperswil, Switzerland, where a museum of Polish national mementoes was established through the efforts of Polish émigrés. After 1927 the urn with Kosciuszko's heart was placed in the chapel of Warsaw's Royal Castle, and during the Nazi occupation period it was removed to Warsaw Cathedral. In 1963 it was moved to one of the rooms of the National Museum of Warsaw, which had been transformed into a mausoleum. At present it is in the Łazienki Palace, whence it will be returned to its former place of enshrinement after the Royal Castle is rebuilt. Photographs of the Royal Castle as it appeared before World War II and during reconstruction (mid-1974)

In the house at Solothurn, where Kosciuszko spent the last two years of his life and died on 15 October 1817, a museum was established in 1936. A plaque unveiled in 1865 is located at the entrance. In the upstairs room where Kosciuszko died a bed covered with a banner stands in an alcove; to the right is the urn in which Kosciuszko's heart was kept at Rapperswil

Kosciuszko

Sans brigue, sans envie, intègre et magnanime
Il sut tout par lui même et dut tout à l'estime

Thaddeus Kosciuszko's ceremonial funeral, marked by the interment of his remains among the sarcophagi of Poland's kings in the crypts of Wawel Cathedral in Cracow, took place in June 1818. A copper engraving, created by a Viennese artist to commemorate the funeral, depicts the catafalque on which the coffin was displayed in Cracow Cathedral. The side walls of the catafalque contain painted scenes of Kosciuszko being decorated by Washington with the American Order of the Cincinnati and the oath of allegiance he took in the Cracow market place on 24 March 1794

The first more extensive biographies of Thaddeus Kosciuszko were the work of foreigners who had personally known the Polish patriot during the final years of his life. A Frenchman, Marc A. Jullien, published his "Notice biographique sur Thaddeus Kosciuszko" in Paris in 1818 (a Polish edition of this book appeared a year later in Wrocław). Karl Falkenstein, published a biography at Leipzig in 1827, a Polish translation of which appeared the same year

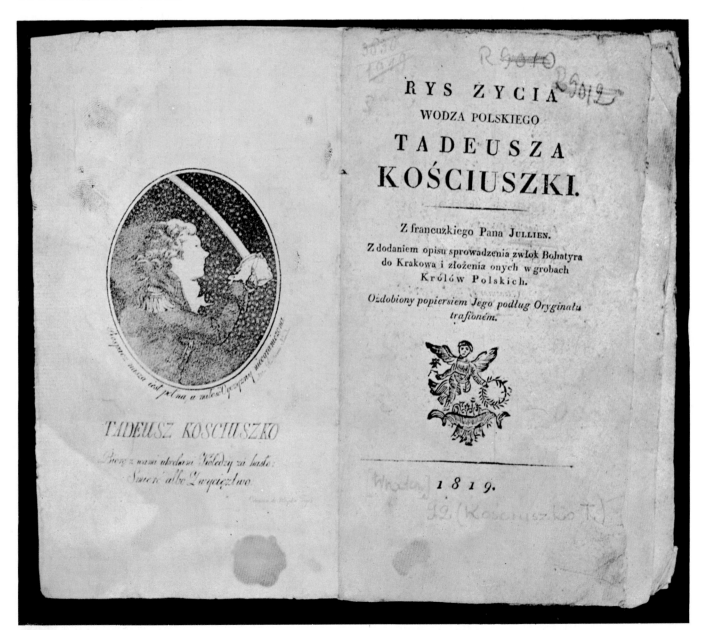

RYS ZYCIA
WODZA POLSKIEGO
TADEUSZA
KOŚCIUSZKI.

Z francuzkiego Pana JULLIEN.

Z dodaniem opisu sprowadzenia zwłok Bohatyra do Krakowa i złożenia onych w grobach Królów Polskich.

Ozdobiony popiersiem Jego podług Oryginału trafioném.

1819.

Tadeusz Kościuszko
Naczelnik siły zbroyney narodowey.
urodz. 1746 um. 1817.

TADEUSZ KOŚCIUSZKO

CZYLI

DOKŁADNY RYS JEGO ŻYCIA

PRZEZ

KAROLA FALKENSTEINA,

Sekretarza przy królestwo-saskiéy publiczney bibliotece w Dreźnie, i członka towarzystwa szwaycarskiego umiejętności.

Cari sunt parentes, cari liberi, propinqui, familiares; sed omnes omnium caritates patria complectitur.
CICERO de officiis.

Z NIEMIECKIEGO NA JĘZYK OYCZYSTY PRZEŁOŻONY.

Z POPIERSIEM BOHATERA PODŁUG ORYGINAŁU TRAFIONÉM.

w WROCŁAWIU,

U WILHELMA BOGUMIŁA KORNA.

1827.

In the years 1820—23 a mound commemorating the hero was created on one of the hills surrounding Cracow. A contemporary drawing depicted the initial phase of the undertaking with earth being placed round the fir-tree trunk that formed the mound's nucleus. Right: the commemorative urn containing the act of authorization which was placed at the base of the mound. Earth from the battlefield of Racławice was brought in an oaken casket on a wagon drawn by four horses in solemn procession and deposited in the mound. Taking part in the cortège were Kosciuszko's former comrades-in-arms who were joined in the streets of Cracow by banner-bearing guild members. That scene was depicted by the painting of Michał Stachowicz. The Kosciuszko Mound upon completion is shown in a lithograph by Maciej Stenczyński

The Kosciuszko Monument in Cracow set against Wawel Cathedral and the sarcophagus of Kosciuszko (in 1818) in the cathedral's crypts. (The sarcophagus of Prince Józef Poniatowski is visible in the background). The monument designed in 1899 was first erected in 1921; destroyed by the Nazis in 1940, it was rebuilt in 1960 as a gift to Cracow from the city of Dresden

W ROKU 1775
MIESZKAŁ W DOMU TYM
TADEUSZ KOSCIUSZKO
NAONCZAS KAPITAN
KORPUSU KADETÓW

TABLICĘ TĘ W MIEJSCE ZNISZCZONEJ ZNISZCZONEJ
PRZEZ NIEMCÓW UFUNDOWAŁ GŁÓWNY KOMITET
KOSCIUSZKOWSKI 1946 ROKU

Numerous sites in Cracow were connected with Kosciuszko's sojourn in that town. A commemorative plaque in the market place marks the house in which he stayed briefly during his first visit to Cracow in 1775. The plaque, unveiled in 1892, was destroyed by the Nazis; a new one was unveiled in its place in 1946. Also in the Cracow market place is the Grey House which served as Kosciuszko's quarters during the early days of the insurrection. On the wall of the Capuchin Church is another plaque commemorating the sword-blessing ceremony in which Kosciuszko, together with the commander of the Cracow garrison, Józef Wodzicki, took part on the morning of 24 March 1794 prior to the official proclamation of the insurrection. The site at which the Supreme Commander took his oath of allegiance is honored by a commemorative tablet. Boy scouts and girl guides of the Thaddeus Kosciuszko Troop now mount honorary guards at the scene on festive occasions

NA TYM MIEJSCU
TADEUSZ KOŚCIUSZKO
PRZYSIĘGAŁ
NARODOWI POLSKIEMU
24 MARCA 1794

KTO Z BOGIEM BÓG Z NIM

TADEUSZ KOŚCIUSZKO

Present-day view of the Kosciuszko Mound whose surroudings were unfortunately blemished by the Austrian fortifications erected in the 19th century. The mound is 34 meters tall and the paths leading to its summit are 316 meters in length. In 1860 a granite boulder from the Tatra Mountains bearing the inscription "To Kosciuszko" was placed at its summit. On the slope of the mound is a plaque marking the spot where earth from the battlefields of the American Revolution was deposited

The countryside near Racławice where the famous battle was fought on 4 April 1794. This site is now marked by a mound

Many Polish military formations were to bear the name of Kosciuszko. That tradition was further enhanced by World War II when the famed 303 fighter squadron which took part in the Battle of Britain in 1940, was named after the hero of Racławice. The emblem of the squadron combined Polish symbols with elements of the American flag.

In Poland there were partisan units of the People's Army named after Thaddeus Kosciuszko and Casimir Pulaski. The Home Army commemorated the 150th anniversary of the Kosciuszko Insurrection with an underground pamphlet signed with a quotation from a 19th-century patriotic hymn.

The best-known formation bearing Kosciuszko's name was the First Infantry Division, formed in 1943 at Seltsy on the Oka in the Soviet Union, which became the nucleus of the First Polish Army, whose battle route led from Lenino to Berlin. Those two names and dates, together with the date 9 May 1945, now grace the badge of the First Thaddeus Kosciuszko Warsaw Infantry Division, an heir to the traditions of the Kosciuszko Division of World War II fame

ŚMIERĆ LUB ZWYCIĘSTWO

1794 24 III 1944

PATRZ KOŚCIUSZKO NA NAS Z NIEBA, TWEGO MIECZA NAM POTRZEBA,
JAK W KRWI WROGÓW BĘDZIEM BRODZIĆ, BY OJCZYZNĘ WYSWOBODZIĆ.

The banner of the First Thaddeus Kosciuszko Infantry Division which accompanied the division from Lenino to Berlin. Today it is on display in the Museum of the Polish Army in Warsaw

300

There are few Polish towns without a street or a square named after Thaddeus Kosciuszko. Monuments in his honor have been erected in many places throughout the country. Besides the one at Wawel, the best known are those located at Łódź and Poznań, (opposite page). Like the Cracow monument, they were destroyed by the Nazis and were rebuilt after the war: the monument at Łódź, erected in 1931, was rebuilt in 1960; the one at Poznań, unveiled in 1930, was reconstructed in 1967

WASHINGTON I KOSCIUSZ

Poland's first transatlantic cargo-vessels, which sailed the Gdynia—New York line between 1931 and 1935 and later serviced the South American line up till 1939, were named after Kosciuszko and Pulaski. They subsequently took part in World War II as transport ships on the Atlantic, Mediterranean and Indian Ocean in the service of the Allied cause.

Kosciuszko is the patron of hundreds of schools and factories, including the foundry at Chorzów

There is an extensive and highly variegated collection of medals bearing the likeness of Thaddeus Kosciuszko. Reproduced are some of those struck between 1817 and 1917

A medal struck in 1946 on the 200th anniversary of Thaddeus Kosciuszko's birth. A medal struck in 1967 by the Polonia Society on the 150th anniversary of Kosciuszko's death

Thaddeus Kosciuszko on banknotes dating from 1919 and on the common 10 zloty piece which has been in circulation since 1957

ZA WOLNOŚĆ WASZĄ I NASZĄ

4.90 ZŁ

GEORGE WASHINGTON

POLSKA

FOR YOUR FREEDOM AND OURS

4.90 ZŁ

TADEUSZ KOŚCIUSZKO

POLSKA

YORKTOWN

4.90 ZŁ

KAZIMIERZ PULASKI

POLSKA

4 ZŁ

POLSKA

KAZIMIERZ PUŁASKI WYBITNY POLAK UCZESTNIK WALK O WOLNOŚĆ AMERYKI

6.40 ZŁ

POLSKA

TADEUSZ KOŚCIUSZKO POLSKI BOHATER NARODOWY WALCZĄCY O WOLNOŚĆ AMERYKI

Among the planes put into service on Poland's first transatlantic Warsaw—New York passenger line in 1974 are jetliners bearing the names of the Polish-American heroes

The illustrations contained in this book attest to the wealth of traditions associated with Kosciuszko and Pulaski. There are far more pictures of Kosciuszko than of Pulaski. At least a hundred paintings and drawings of Kosciuszko were produced during his lifetime. Some of them were faithful portrayals meriting full confidence, whilst others mainly reflected the fanciful imagination of their creators. As the leader of the insurrection Kosciuszko was a widely known and respected figure. Pulaski, by contrast, did not gain widespread fame until after his death, hence not a single contemporary portrait of him has been discovered. Moreover, far fewer mementoes of the more than four-year-long period of confederate struggle have survived than of the 200-day Kosciuszko Insurrection.

In compiling illustrative material related to Kosciuszko and Pulaski all available Polish sources have been probed. These include memorabilia which had the good fortune to survive the ravages of war, mainly from the National Museum and the Polish Army Museum in Warsaw, the National Museum in Cracow, the Cracow Historical Museum and the Casimir Pulaski Museum at Warka. Unfortunately, not all American collections could be fully taken advantage of. Hence, despite the extensive illustrations contained in this book, it cannot be said that all materials meriting presentation have been included.

This fact notwithstanding, it should be mentioned that the vast amount of such material (particularly in regard to Kosciuszko) made stringent selection necessary. Various criteria were used: documentary value, aesthetic considerations and often merely the attractiveness of certain illustrations, devoid of historical or artistic value in themselves, but indicative of the traditions and imagination of their authors.

Scanning the panorama of illustrations here presented one should not only seek factual knowledge, but also manifestations of tradition and legend which have their place in history too. Indeed they have often served as an attractive starting point for those who take pleasure in exploring the past. I hope this book will be a starting point for those who wish to find out about Thaddeus Kosciuszko and Casimir Pulaski.

List of illustrations

The dates of birth and death of artists are provided only when the absence of other biographical information makes it impossible to determine the period in which their works appeared.

Abbreviations:

ADM — Mechanical Documentation Archives in Warsaw
BCK — Czartoryski Library in Cracow
BJ — Jagiellonian Library
BNW — National Library in Warsaw
BUW — Warsaw University Library
FMW — J.J. Michalski Foundation in Warsaw
IS PAN — Institute of Art of the Polish Academy of Sciences in Warsaw
MHK — Cracow Historical Museum
MKP — Kazimierz Pulaski Museum at Warka
MNK — National Museum in Cracow
MNL — National Museum in Lublin
MNP — National Museum in Poznań
MNW — National Museum in Warsaw
MWP — Polish Army Museum in Warsaw

Jacket: A medal with the likenesses of Thaddeus Kosciuszko and Casimir Pulaski, struck on the 150th anniversary of the US Declaration of Independence

Front-paper: Drawing of eagle done in 1807 by Aleksander Orłowski

317

Polish Editor: Wanda Michalak

Translated by Robert Strybel

Production Editor: Grzegorz Bielawski

Photographs by

T. Barucki, Central Photographic Agency, A. Chiczewski, M. Ciunowicz, S. Deptuszewski,
F. Fabjaniak, J. Fil, Z. Gamski, E. Haneman, H. Hermanowicz, A. A. Iszczuk, W. P. Jabłoński,
E. Kozłowska-Tomczyk, R. Kreyser, J. Langda, M. Kobrzyński, Z. Malinowski, S. Moszuk
A. Mottl, F. Maćkowiak, L. Perz, Polish Interpress Agency, Rakowski, H. Romanowski,
S. Sobkowicz, T. Trepanowski, J. Werner and L. Zielaskowski

Designed by Jerzy Kępkiewicz

Illustrations selected by Jan Stanisław Kopczewski

PRINTED IN POLAND

This book appears also in Polish

This is the one thousand five hundred and forty-ninth publication of Interpress

Ilustrations printed by
ZAKŁADY WKLĘSŁODRUKOWE RSW „PRASA-KSIĄŻKA-RUCH" — WARSZAWA

Printed and bound at
PRASOWE ZAKŁADY GRAFICZNE RSW „PRASA-KSIĄŻKA-RUCH" — BYDGOSZCZ